I0473465

Book Marketing That Drives Up Book Sales:
Sell via Bookstores, Book Tours, Radio, Exchanges & More

Copyright 2020

Chistell Publishing

First Printing, January 2021

Published by: Chistell Publishing
                       7235 Aventine Way, Suite #201
                       Chattanooga, TN 37421

ISBN: 978-0-9663539-7-6

Dedication

For my son.

I love you, Gregory –

Acknowledgements

Appreciation to the Source of eternal creation.

Thank you to my family. My father, Richard Turney. My mother, Doris Jean. My son, Gregory. My grandparents, Clyde and Emma Turney. My great-grandmother Rebecca Skinner. My brothers, Richard, Clark and Eric. My sister – Adrianne. My nephew and nieces, Richard, Angel, Assyria, Samaria, Megan, and John. My aunts, Christine and Pat. My uncle Donald. My great-aunt Ruby. My cousins Donna, Monica, Michael and Langston. Thank you for a foundation of love.

To my friends and supporters. To those who read, support and enjoy my books. To my Sigma Gamma Rho sorors. To Tim and Essie Stackhouse, a woman who God used to allow the story of Ruth and Naomi to work itself into my own life. To Helen Crawford (I'll never forget you walking around the corner those many times just to see how I was doing).

To everyone who has touched my life in a special way, including each person who has read my books, thank you for your love and support.

Be courageous and wonderful, loving YOU! -- Denise

Preface

Writing a book is a significant time investment. As an author, you've either developed fictional characters, plot, dialogue and imaginary settings, working them into an intriguing novel, or you've researched and interpreted analytics, raw data, articles and recorded interviews to develop an informative nonfiction book. Congratulations! What you did is no small feat.

Now, it's time to find your book's readers. It's time to sell your book. Book Marketing That Drives Up Book Sales aims to help you do just that - sell books.

After more than 30 years in the book industry, I've learned quite a bit about selling books, including what works and what doesn't.

Not only does Book Marketing That Drives Up Book Sales cover how to find success on book tours and how to land podcasts and radio interviews, within the pages of Book Marketing That Drives Up Book Sales, you'll find podcasts directories, press release distribution services, book ad companies, places to market writing blogs, how to tap into exchanges and non-bookstore markets and more.

There's years of firsthand experience and research within these pages. In fact, I wish that someone had told me what I'm going to share with you years ago. It would have saved me countless hours of work and thousands of dollars. As a bonus, <u>Book Marketing That Drives Up Book Sales</u> covers online and offline book marketing.

As a tip, even as you read <u>Book Marketing That Drives Up Book Sales</u>, continue to learn, keep trying different book marketing techniques, resources and strategies. After all, advancing technology will see new book marketing apps, tools and resources develop.

And, despite the fact that it doesn't involve the actual process of sitting down and writing a book, marketing books is a process that you may come to love, especially as you start receiving fruit from your labor. Follow guidance in <u>Book Marketing That Drives Up Book Sales</u> and you could save years of frustration. Better yet, you could sell lots of books.

Book Marketing That Drives Up Book Sales:

Sell via Bookstores, Book Tours, Radio, Exchanges & More

You already have everything inside of you that you need to succeed!

TABLE OF CONTENTS

Book Marketing That Drives Up Book Sales **Page**

"If there's a book that you want to read, but it hasn't been written yet, then you must write it."
-- Toni Morrison

Chapter 1 - Why Did You Write Your Book?

At the core of connecting with readers and selling books rest the answer to the question - why did you write your book? And there may be more than one answer to this question.

For instance, did you write your book to sell enough copies to afford to switch careers, becoming a full-time novelist? Or did you write your book to inspire teens living in foster care?

You may have written your book to establish yourself as an industry expert, to use as a giveaway at trade shows or to introduce prospects to your company's products and services.

The answer to your question will help determine your target audience. It should also drive content that you *keep* in your book. And it will align your book to one or more genres. If you wrote your book to intrigue or to frighten readers, you're going to have to find readers who love a mystery or a psychological thriller.

On the other hand, if you want to teach children math skills, you'll have to revert to technical writing. You'll also have to market to a different audience than you'd market a psychological thriller to.

Also, as tempting as it may feel, avoid falling into the trap of thinking that your book is for *everyone*. And okay. Depending on your book's price, anyone *could* buy and read the book, regardless of the topic. But not everyone *wants* to read your book, simply because not everyone is interested in your book's topic or genre.

Another reason to get clear about why you wrote your book is linked to reward. If you wrote your book to offer techniques that help adults practice self-love and readers tell you that they started meditating, exercising, resting and setting clear guidelines with colleagues and relatives after they read your book, that would feel satisfying. You would have achieved your goal for *why* you wrote your book.

Each time that you're rewarded for your *why* (the reason that you wrote your book), you'll be encouraged. You'll feel energized to continue your book marketing efforts.

Here are several questions that may help you to get clear about why you wrote your book. Take your time. Answers to these questions may pop up throughout your book marketing efforts.

- What do you want readers to gain from reading your book (e.g. romantic sparks, inspiration, learn a skill)?
- Of all the book genres, which is your favorite to read?
- Do you plan to use your book as a make-shift business card (or as a way to introduce your company to prospects)?
- Are you writing to sell enough books to work as a full-time novelist?
- Is your main reason for writing a book to express yourself?
- As a ghostwriter, have you been hired to write a book for a client?
- Have you written your book to capture your family history?

- Would you like to honor someone by focusing on her or him in the book?

After you identify why you wrote your book, it's time to revisit the manuscript. Be patient. There are several actions to check off before you publish your book. We'll only touch on those actions briefly. But they are critical to your book's success.

If you've already written and published your book, consider returning to this chapter should you decide to write another book. After all, the *whys* behind desire, intent and action are important.

"Write what should not be forgotten."
-- Isabel Allende

Chapter 2 - Book Quality Matters A Lot

Get clear about why you want to write a book and write in a genre or about a topic that you're passionate about, and you could have the fuel to craft a bestseller. Even if you're not a literary writer, someone who may spend years crafting and polishing a novel, that doesn't mean that top quality shouldn't be your aim.

If this is your first book, steer yourself free of thinking that the book is fabulous simply because you wrote it. In fact, test the quality of your late drafts. Join a writer's critique group.

Go for writers' critique groups that have a mix of members. Some members should be new writers, other members should be experienced, published authors, people who have been publishing and marketing books for five years or longer. Share book chapters with group members. Accept honest feedback.

It's an effective way to identify parts of your story that need to be tightened, deleted or polished. Continue to edit-edit-edit.

After the second edit, step away from the manuscript for two weeks. Return to the manuscript and do another read-through and edit.

Next, consider working with beta readers. These are people who are avid readers of the genre that your novel is in. Writing a nonfiction book? Work with beta readers who have read several books that your manuscript's topic is on.

This may bear repeating. Accept honest feedback. You don't have to incorporate all of the feedback into your manuscript. But, if five beta readers tell you that the pace of your novel is too slow, you should pay attention.

After all, you're trying to write your best book, not protect or defend your ego. When you feel that your book is near ready for publication, do a spell check. Depending on your software (e.g. Word), you might also be able to run a grammar check. This step completed, it's time to focus on your book's logistics.

ISBN, Copyright and LCCN

Publishers generally handle applying for an International Standard Book Number (ISBN) for a new book. Self-published authors handle getting an ISBN assigned for their books. To get an ISBN, you can hop over to Bowker (http://www.bowker.com/authors). Identify the country that you want to get your ISBN in. Click "Learn More" and follow the prompts.

As a tip, if you plan on publishing several books, consider buying a bulk number of ISBNs. One ISBN costs $125. However, you can get 10 ISBNs for $295, as of the first printing of Book Marketing That Drives Up Book Sales.

Copyright Protection

Register your book for copyright early. Each country has its own copyright process. There is no international copyright office. Furthermore, should you need to go to court, having a registered copyright offers protection. Also, according to the United States Copyright Office, "as a general rule, for works created after January 1, 1978, copyright protection lasts for the life of the author plus an additional 70 years."[1]

As a heads up, it takes about 10 minutes to register a copyright. Here's the U.S. Copyright office registration link: https://www.copyright.gov/registration.

Log into the U.S. Copyright office's digital platform. You'll have to register if this is your first time accessing the system. Once registered, select "Literary Works" for the type of registration that you want.

Follow the prompts on the screen. The fee to register a single author work is $45 as of the first printing of Book Marketing That Drives Up Book Sales. You can pay the fee electronically. When your book is published, send two (2) copies to the U.S. Copyright office.

Library of Congress Control Number (LCCN)
To register your book with the Library of Congress, go to: https://www.loc.gov/publish/pcn. There is no cost to register for a LCCN.

The LCCN is used by librarians to identify your book. Here's how the Library of Congress states it, "The principal intention of the PCN Program is to assign Library of Congress Control Numbers (LCCNs) in advance of publication to those titles that the Library may add to its collections. When printed in the book, the LCCN facilitates access to the bibliographic record for that book and thereby expedites book processing by libraries and book dealers who obtain copies of the book."[2]

Please note that, according to the Library of Congress, "There is no charge for a Preassigned Control Number (PCN). However, participating publishers are obligated to send a complimentary copy of all books for which a Preassigned Control Number (PCN) was provided immediately upon publication." Also, please note that, "Publishers failing to meet this obligation may be suspended from the program. Please note that all books submitted to the Library of Congress in compliance with the PCN Program are property of the Library of Congress and therefore are not returnable."[2]

Feel free to register your book with the Copyright office and to register for an ISBN and LCCN when your book nears publication. What you may not want to delay is finding and working with an experienced and talented book editor.

Working With Experienced Editors

Start working with an editor *after* you have done several rounds of self-editing. It may be a good idea to wait to work with an editor until after you've received feedback from beta readers and members of a writer's critique group. This way, you can incorporate that feedback into your manuscript prior to handing the manuscript to an editor.

A traditional publisher may assign an editor to review your manuscript. You'll handle this item yourself as a self-published author.

Here's a tip. Don't focus solely on price when selecting an editor. Choose an editor who you'll enjoy working with over the course of your career (unless you only plan to publish one book).

Also, go with an editor who has deep experience editing the types of books that you write. For instance, some editors work with children's books. Other editors specialize in romance novels or nonfiction science textbooks.

Another factor to consider is whether you want someone to line edit your work or offer feedback on story development. With line editing, an editor will check spelling, grammar, that a character is wearing braces in chapter one and no braces in chapter three without mention of the character visiting the dentist to have the braces removed, etc.

An editor who's hired to look at story development will offer feedback on plot, dialogue, character development, pacing and story arc. Price ranges for book editors vary. For example, some editors charge $20 an hour, while others charge $25 or more an hour.

Then, you may find editors who charge by the page. In this case, an editor might charge $5 or $7 a page. You can do an online search for an experienced editor. Or you can ask authors who publish books similar to yours to recommend an editor.

Do your homework. The editor is working for you. Check references. Also, ask the editor to share titles of published books that he or she has already edited. Read through parts of those books. This way, you can get a feel for the editor's results.

Here are more places where you could find experienced book editors to work with:

- **Reedsy** - www.reedsy.com
- **Fiverr** - www.fiverr.com
- **Kindlepreneur** - https://kindlepreneur.com/book-editors
- **Book Buzzr** - https://bookbuzzr.com/blog/directory-of-book-editing-services/

LinkedIn is another place where you could find an experienced editor. Interview editors before you make a final decision. Even more, find a good editor who becomes familiar with your work, and you could cut the time that it takes to get a book ready for publication. You might also develop a good friendship, red ink, strike-thrus and all.

Advantages of Working with Book Editors
In case you're still on the fence about working with an experienced book editor, consider that the marriage between book writers and book editors might be one of the most complex relationships around. If you've ever worked full-time as a writer or editor, you probably know what I mean. As a book writer, you might think that your work is excellent, certainly not worthy of an

editor's criticisms. Yet, that's where you are likely to always be wrong.

Zoning in on Talented Book Editors' Trained Eyes

In fact, there might not be a *perfect* book, especially to a talented book editor's trained eye. When they're working on a book, editors look for grammatical errors, voice inconsistencies, awkward tone and style, to start. Book editors also examine characterization, dialogue, setting and plot. Because they are trained to look for and zone in on elements authors might ignore, book editors notice weaknesses in stories that authors don't. This could be a reason why some authors get upset when they receive an editor's feedback.

More Advantages to Working With Book Editors

The funny thing is, it's nearly impossible to avoid receiving feedback on a book if you're an author. Think about it. If talented book editors, people who have the best interest of your book at heart, don't offer you feedback, book reviewers and readers almost certainly will. Unfortunately, when book reviewers and readers spot weaknesses in your books, they may not be as kind or as gentle as editors. Unlike editors, reviewers and readers also might tell others about the weaknesses in your stories, costing you book sells.

Other advantages inherit in working with book editors include:

- Smoother scene transitions
- Fewer to no typos or misspelled words
- More believable book characters
- Strong, realistic dialogue
- Improved timing and pacing
- A workable number of characters instead of too many or too few book characters

Book editors offer critical feedback. Their work can help turn an average story into an above average story. Furthermore, as writers continue to work with the same editors, the pairs can form rewarding relationships. They could also become familiar with each other's style and come to fully respect what each brings to the creative table. It's a marriage that's worth fighting for.

"Book marketing should be a planned process, an art if you will." -- Heather Hart

Chapter 3 - Book Marketing Is Ongoing

Book marketing is a marathon. You may have heard this stated about book writing as well. Even if you stack book marketing campaigns to boost sales of a new book, you'll have to setup additional marketing actions to *keep* your books in front of readers.

And now that your manuscript is registered for copyright, has an ISBN and LCCN and has been under the careful eye of an experienced editor, it's time to get down to the art of book marketing.

Over the next several chapters, we'll cover book tours, radio interviews, getting on podcasts, what to expect while on television, social media marketing, bookstore and non-bookstore marketing and more. But first I want to impress upon you that successful book marketing is not a one-time gig.

Successful book marketing is an ongoing process. In fact, *New York Times* bestselling authors market their books.

Think about it. Even major actresses and actors get out and do television interviews to market and promote their new movies. These are household names A-List actresses and actors.

Major recording artists do the same, adding in sell-out concert tours. The point is to stay in front of your audience.

Do what it takes to stay in your reading audience's awareness. Thanks to technology and resources and techniques shared in <u>Book Marketing That Drives Up Book Sales</u>, you can pull quite a bit of this off while you're sleeping.

As an author, do you love sharing stories with readers? Is writing a passion for you? Are you determined to find and connect with your book's audience?

If you answered yes, get ready to explore the art of book marketing. And get ready to go on a book marketing journey that will put you in contact with influencers, social media personalities, offline media pros and avid book readers.

"You can't expect to write and have visitors come to you - that's too passive." -- Anita Campbell

Chapter 4 - About Book Tours

Book marketing starts four to six months *before* your book is published. But you can still gain good traction even if you don't start marketing your book until after it's published. Part of this work includes a book tour.

Also, years ago, if you were sent on a book tour, you might visit television stations, conduct radio interviews and attend public speaking and book signing events in 24 to 30 different cities. Day one may start with an in-person interview at a major, local radio station, then extend to a book reading and book signing at one to two bookstores with lunch at a corporation before or after you deliver a speech that's related to your book.

Following lunch, you might be whisked to a book conference where you'd sit on a panel for Q&A. That evening, you might do another radio station interview or another bookstore signing. And that's just Day One.

At first glance, it sounds sexy, exciting. But, somewhere between home and the 10th city, you start to feel jet lagged, fatigued with being "up" and the pressure to earn back the money that the publisher is spending on your hotels, transportation and meals, if those are included in your travel and expenses (T&E).

On the other hand, if you love public speaking and connecting with readers in person, you might get a boost from a book tour. Just be prepared to juggle a tight schedule.

In-Person Book Tours
Land a book contract with a traditional publisher, and they'll handle the book tour for you. However, publishers have cut back on book tours since the Great Recession, some prior to the Recession. But that doesn't mean that your publisher won't schedule a book tour for you.

Expect to be assigned a handler or an escort. This person may reside in the city that you're visiting. She'll ensure that you get to events on time. She may also get light meals for you. To get more out of the book tour, bring your laptop or iPad with you. At night, conduct online marketing by visiting your social media accounts and posting videos and pictures of your book tour events.

You might even start on a new novel (dare you have the energy). Just remember that your goal is to sell books, engage new readers to expand your audience and strengthen your brand as an author. In other words, don't get caught up in the hype and the noise. Stay focused on your goal even as you have fun meeting and connecting with readers.

Here's another point. Should your publisher not schedule you for a book tour, that doesn't stop you from arranging your own in-person book tour. The same applies if you're a self-published author.

There are two options, you can foot the entire bill or work with event organizers to see if they'll pay for your hotel or transportation. To build your own in-person book tour, create a budget for the tour. Create a daily budget, a weekly budget and an overall budget for the tour. Stick to this budget.

Save time by creating your budget on a spreadsheet. (I'm big on tracking ROI on spreadsheets). Items to include in your book tour budget are:

- Transportation (e.g. airfare, rental car, taxi/Uber/Lyft)
- Hotels
- Meals
- Emergency Funds (e.g. last minute travel changes, clothes in the event your luggage gets lost)
- Hygiene items

In-Person Book Tour Itinerary
Budget developed, sit down and map out your daily schedule. Here's an example of how you could fill out your daily itinerary:

- **6am** - Breakfast
- **7am** - Local in-station radio interview (share your website URL during every radio interview)
- **9am** - Podcast interview (you could do this from your hotel room)
- **9:30am** - 2nd Podcast interview
- **11am** - Bookstore reading or lecture followed by a 20-30 minute book signing
- **12:30pm** - Lunch
- **1:30pm** - Panel discussion at citywide book festival or writer's conference (If you were asked to attend the

event, ask the event organizer's if they will pay you a speaker's fee or pick up the cost of your hotel and/or airfare.)

- **4:30pm** - Head to the airport to travel to the next city on the book tour

It's up to you to schedule radio and podcasts interviews. As a tip, if in-person radio DJs like you, they could ask you to return, helping you to build a new audience of readers. Should you be asked back, ask if you can knock out the second radio interview over the phone.

Also, research radio stations to ensure that your book is a fit for their audience. The best way to do this is to listen to the radio shows that you're interested in being interviewed on. Get familiar with the format, the DJ's personality and the types of questions that DJs and listeners ask.

Note: Radio station resources are listed in the Book Tour Resources section at the end of this chapter.

In-Person Book Tour Expenses
A good way to limit your book tour expenses is to travel to cities that are within easy driving distance. This is the

approach that I took when I first promoted my debut novel, <u>Portia</u>. I booked events up and down the United States' eastern shore. Talk about reserving rental cars. Was I ever on the road.

Of course, if you own a good vehicle, you could save on rental car and airline expenses and just drive to events that are within 200 to 300 miles of where you live. Just tie the trips to book festivals and book conferences. Also, schedule two to three local in-person radio interviews when you visit the cities. Boost the marketing with at least one local television interview.

As a tip, public television stations may be more willing to interview you, especially if you're a local author. Arrive to television stations at least 30 minutes before the show starts. Dress professionally. Sit tall and relax. Also, answer questions with open ended responses. A good television interviewer will guide you and may send you questions that he plans to ask prior to the show.

Below are more events that you could add to your in-person book tour:

- Library speaking events

- Local book club visits
- College and university literary events
- Meetings with local newspaper and local magazine journalists
- Appearances at small businesses that offer products or services that align with your book's topic

Develop a daily itinerary for each day of your book tour. Fill in hourly slots. Try to fill up the day to get the most traction from the tour.

Align the daily schedule with your daily budget. For example, you could map out a day that shows:

- Hotel (*Paid for by Book Festival you're a panelist for*)
- **6am** - Breakfast (*$10 or less - Pay for yourself*)
- **7am** - Local in-station radio interview (share your website URL during every radio interview) - (*Uber at $40 max roundtrip*)
- **9am** - Podcast interview (you could do this from your hotel room)
- **9:30am** - 2nd Podcast interview
- **11am** - Bookstore reading or lecture followed by a 20-30 minute book signing (*Lyft at $20 max roundtrip*)
- **12pm** - Lunch (*$15 or less - pay for yourself*)

- **1pm** - Panel discussion at citywide book festival or writer's conference. You could save on hotel costs by staying at an AirnB or by staying at a friend's or relative's who lives in the city that you're visiting.) - (*Taxi pickup and drop-off / Paid for by Book Festival organizers*)
- **4pm** - Head to the airport to travel to the next city on the book tour (*Take free hotel shuttle to airport*) - (*Budget $400 roundtrip - pay for yourself. Of course, if you drive your own car, you won't have this expense.*)

Consider using money that you get from book festival, bookstore and book club signing sales to pay for future book editing, book cover design, etc. costs. Also, use the money to pay quarterly business taxes and invest in your personal savings.

Online Book Tours
Online book tours involve phone radio interviews, book reviews, podcasts interviews, digital television interviews, feature blog interviews and live Q&A video sessions.

Prior to 2020 (the year of COVID19 and social distancing), authors were taking advantage of technology, connecting with book buyers and bringing their book tours online. However, online virtual events picked up significantly during 2020.

Although you won't have to deal with hotels and transportation while on digital book tours, there is scheduling to knock out. And you could incur expenses if you hire an online book tour company. For example, there are companies that coordinate online book tours, taking on interview scheduling, giveaways and Q&A. Also, quality online book tour coordinators have direct connections with radio stations, book reviewers, digital television stations, podcast hosts and popular book bloggers.

These connections can save you hours of work. In other words, you won't have to search for radio stations, podcasts, book bloggers, etc. to reach out to in order to schedule interviews. Coordinators will handle this legwork for you.

Key online book tour features include:
- Start and end dates for the book tour

- Interviewer name and contact information
- Specific dates and times for each interview
- Radio / podcasts dial in directions
- Written questions for feature print interviews
- Dates for live Facebook, etc. interviews

To do this legwork yourself, revisit *why* you wrote your book. If you wrote a mystery to intrigue, entertain and suspend reader imagination, search for book reviewers, podcasts, radio stations and book blogs that spotlight mystery books.

Some book bloggers post the types of books that they read/review/conduct author interviews for at their website. Other bloggers post how to submit ARCs and books for consideration to them. Still, you may find book bloggers who note that they are not currently accepting new books.

Don't let this stop you from reaching out to other book bloggers and book reviewers. And don't let a poor book review stop you from book marketing.

In fact, schedule three to five interviews a week. For example, you could schedule three podcasts interviews and two blog interviews one week. Another week, you could schedule two Facebook live interviews, two blog reviews and one digital television interview.

Build out your book tour schedule until it covers three months. Another option is to leave your online book tour end date open. This way, you can keep reaching new book buyers.

As a tip, track each book tour contact on a spreadsheet. Did I tell you that I'm big on tracking results on spreadsheets?

Trust me, you can return to this list of contacts with each new book that you publish and market. Over time, your spreadsheet might come to have more than 500 contacts.

Send book reviewers and book bloggers advanced reader copies (ARCs) pre-publication, the sooner, the better. To save time when contacting book bloggers, book reviewers, podcasts and radio hosts, create a template letter or email that you will send to these contacts.

Yet don't just copy and paste the letter to each contact. Address emails to each person by name. Personalization goes a long way when marketing and promoting. Track the date that you reach out to contacts on your spreadsheet.

Follow-up on emails that you send, after a week. After two follow-ups, wait a month before you reach out to contacts again. Also, add contacts to your holiday mailings (more about that later).

Book Tour Resources
And, now for those book tour resources. Some of these resources may be helpful for online and offline book tours. Resources that are online or offline only, are noted. Of course, you can also use Facebook, Twitter and Instagram hashtags #bookbloggers, #bookreviewers to find bloggers and reviewers to help market your books.

Places to Find Online Book Bloggers
- Book Blogger List - www.bookbloggerlist.com
- Indie Review - www.theindiereview.com
- Book Review Blogs - https://blog.feedspot.com/bookreview_blogs

- Diverse Book Bloggers - https://diversebookbloggersdirectory.wordpress.com/diverse-book-bloggers/

Places to Find Book Reviewers
- Book Review Yellow Pages - https://bookrevieweryellowpages.com
- Book Sirens - https://booksirens.com/book-reviewer-directory
- AALBC - https://aalbc.com

Virtual Book Tours Info
- Oprah Magazine - https://www.oprahmag.com/entertainment/a33902384/authors-virtual-book-tour-experience/
- Writer's Digest - https://www.writersdigest.com/getting-published/13-lessons-epic-book-tour

Book Tour Companies / Bookstore Events (*Do your homework - I am not affiliated with any of these companies, nor am I recommending their services.*)
- WNL - http://wnlbooktours.com/virtual-tour-packages/

- Rock Star Book Tours - http://www.rockstarbooktours.com/p/authors-and-publishers.html
- Barnes & Noble - https://www.barnesandnobleinc.com/publishers-authors/how-to-be-considered-for-an-author-event/
- Poets & Writers - https://www.pw.org/reading_venues
- Lit Hub - https://lithub.com/literary-hub-presents-the-virtual-book-channel/
- C-SPAN - https://www.c-span.org/about/faq/
- TLC - https://tlcbooktours.com/

Author Podcasts Directories
- FM Podcasts - https://player.fm/podcasts/Book-Author-Interview
- Electric Literature - https://electricliterature.com/eight-excellent-literary-podcasts-for-your-morning-commute/
- The Write Life - https://thewritelife.com/writing-podcasts/

Travel Apps
- Smarter Travel - https://www.smartertravel.com/best-trip-planner-apps/

- Trip It - https://www.tripit.com/web
- Lounge Buddy - https://www.loungebuddy.com/mobile

"Every writer needs a home, an official space to call her own." -- Denise Turney

Chapter 5 - Building an Author Website

This is listed as Chapter 5. However, you should develop an official author website before you start contacting book bloggers, reviewers and media to do a book tour.

There are several reasons to have an official author website. Media contacts, newsletter editors and book bloggers will reference your website when researching questions to ask you during interviews.

Even more, book buyers may visit your official author website to learn more about your writing background, your hobbies and what inspired you to start writing. Sharing basic information with website visitors is a way to build trust.

And it's trust that builds the bridge from readers learning about you and your books to readers buying your books. But, just what does an effective author's website consist of? To begin, a good website is desktop _and_ mobile friendly. A good author's website also has the following features:

- **Landing Page** - A single page that comes up when people conducting an online search click on a link. This page is generally static, meaning that its content doesn't change. Examples of a landing page are a book order page, newsletter sign up page or a book catalog page. Purpose of a landing page is to trigger a specific call-to-action (CTA).
- **Main Page** - Include the cover of your latest book. Also, add links to your author bio, media info, books page, newsletter sign-up, podcast, upcoming events and one to three other pages that let visitors learn more about you and your writing endeavors.
- **Books Page** - On this page, include the cover of each of your books. To promote new books, you could post their covers on this page and start sharing the cover, building interest in the book before it is published.
- **Individual Book Pages** - Also, create a separate web page at your official author website for each of your books. For example, if you go to www.chistell.com, you will see a page for each of the books. On these individual book pages is an excerpt, the book cover and a link to order the book.
- **Newsletter Sign-Up Page** - Offer readers the chance to keep in touch with you by creating a literary

newsletter. Make it easy for your website visitors to sign up for your newsletter by allowing them to click a link on your main page that takes them to an opt-in subscription form. More about literary newsletters further into <u>Book Marketing That Drives Up Book Sales</u>.

- **Author Bio** - Strongly consider only sharing basic information online. For example, you could share your name, the region of the world that you live in or the part of the country that you reside in. You might also share what inspired you to start writing books, your college or university major and the names of your favorite authors. Other facts to share on your bio page include your favorite quotes, your writing process and the book that you're currently writing. Include a professional head shot. Some authors also include a quality picture of them engaged in an activity that they love (e.g. running, bike riding, fishing). This second picture could potentially strengthen the connection that visitors have with you.

- **Order Page** - You could post a link to the retailer that you sell the most books through (e.g. Kobo, Google Books, Amazon, Cushcity, Mahogany Books, Amazon). Or you could set up a check-out counter using software like Shopify, PayPal, Stripe or SquareUp and encourage visitors to buy your books directly from you. Also, post the prices for each of your books. As a tip, the price that you set for your book can make a significant impact on book sales. Avoid pricing your book too low. And don't over price your book. Research the prices on ebooks, print books and audio books similar to yours. Factor in the cost to make each copy of the book, including shipping costs. If sales drag, run a discount on the book and see if sales pick up. Pricing a book is more an art than a science. But, as you publish more books, you'll likely discover what works for you.

- **Blog Link** - Definitely include a link to your blog on your official author website. More about blogs as a strong marketing tool further into <u>Book Marketing That Drives Up Book Sales</u>.
- **Contact Info** - Add a contact form to your website so visitors can reach you.

Check out several author websites to see which designs work best. Also, make sure to include a few *New York Times* bestselling author websites in this review. Why?

These authors may have a team of marketing professionals working with them, people who have an undergraduate or graduate marketing education. On a full-time basis, these marketing pros learn how to use new marketing tools, analyze trends and work with design and content to generate book sales.

Just think of your favorite bestselling authors and hop over to their websites. See what you find. You may learn about more tips and features to add to your website.

But, be warned. You don't want to add every good feature to your official author website. Why?

Visitor attention span is short. In fact, as little as five years ago, you could keep visitors at your website for an average of 30 to 45 seconds. As of the first printing of <u>Book Marketing That Drives Up Book Sales</u>, the average time that visitors spend on a website is less than 15 seconds.[3]

Keep your author website uncluttered and quick to download. This means you may not be able to fill the page with videos. Remember, you have a short amount of time to engage visitors.

And, just as you need to remember *why* you started writing, it's rewarding to remember *why* you want people to visit your website. Generally, you want readers to visit your website to learn more about you and your books and to *buy* your books.

When media pros visit your website, you may want them to include you in an article, blog posts or reach out and ask you to do a feature interview. Even more, you may want book club members, librarians and booksellers to ask about including your titles at their libraries, bookstores or book club meetings.

Tracking Website Performance
For these reasons, make sure that your website is performing well after it's designed. You can do this by setting up Google Analytics for your website.

It's as easy as visiting Google Analytics, creating an account and following Google's web stat instructions. As a tip, you or your website designer will have to add a code to each of your website pages that you want Google to track visitor stats for. It's free to add Google Analytics to your website.

Types of activities that Google Analytics tracks include:

- Number of unique visitors
- Number of repeat visitors
- Bounce rate (strive for a low bounce rate)
- Pages that people enter your website on (e.g. author bio, book page)
- Pages that people exit your website on (you may want to enhance these pages or make it faster to scroll these pages to reduce the exits)
- Average time that visitors spend at your website
- Parts of the world that visitors are from

You can also set up a Conversions Tracker via Google Analytics to track how many people click on book order pages. For example, you could set up a tracker to get stats for the number of times visitors click on your first book's order page and your second and third books' order pages.

Google Analytics will report on each separate book order page. Another thing that you can review thru Google Analytics is how many people are active or actually visiting your page when you log into Google Analytics.

Working with Experienced Website Designers

Upwork and Fiverr are places where you could find an affordable website designer. LinkedIn, Facebook and Twitter are other resources that could put you in contact with an experienced website designer. This is someone who understands code, designs a page that loads fast, a person who backs up your content and someone who knows how to work with online order systems (e.g. Shopify, PayPal, Stripe or SquareUp, Due, Apple Pay).

A good website designer is also easy to reach. So, take your time searching for a quality website designer. Also, interview website designers to make sure that yours and the designer's personalities work well together.

Here's a quick overview of what to look for in a website designer. You'll also find tips on working with a website designer below.

Finding the Right Website Designer
Budget - Determine amount you can spend on the design
Explore - Check out websites that the designer has built
Clients - Ask for client testimonials
Costs - Review the designers price options
Hosting - See if the designer offers website hosting
Availability - Get the designer's working hours
Updates - Find out if you can make updates to your website

This bears repeating. Add a type of analytics to your website. Some hosting companies offer website analytics at no additional cost.

Also, in addition to finding a website designer, you'll need to host or park your website on a server. Companies that host websites are called hosting sites or hosting companies.

Find a Website Hosting Company
Fortunately, a good website designer should be able to recommend a hosting company. But the choice of which hosting company to go with is up to you.

When choosing a website hosting company (e.g. Bluehost, Host Gator, Dreamhost), pay attention to the features offered by the hosting company (e.g. analytics, content management system, marketing tools). Also, review downtimes that websites hosted by the company experience.

Other website hosting features that you may want include:

- Unlimited bandwidth
- Free Private SSL
- Unlimited email addresses

- User friendly cPanel
- Website builder templates
- Free website migration
- SPAM Protection
- Forums
- Shopping Cart
- Firewall protection
- Low monthly pricing
- 24/7 customer service

As you start searching for a website designer, deciding which features you want at your website and finding a website hosting company, keep in mind that you can always redesign your website. In fact, it's recommended that you do redesign your website once a year or once every three years.

Just make sure that your website uploads fast. Also, strive for an uncluttered, appealing look. And give visitors enough information to keep them coming back.

One more thing. If you have website design skills, you could use tools like WordPress, Wix or Web Easy to design your own website. But, if you don't have strong website design skills, it's good to leave that to the pros.

"Marketing is not a one-time thing. It is an ongoing process that you must keep doing to continue selling books." -- Sarah Bolme

Chapter 6 - Blogging to Attract Readers

Blogging not only keeps your author website current, it's an effective way to attract new readers. In fact, blogs are so good at pulling in traffic, major corporations hire blog writers.

But here's the rub. As an author, it can become tempting to blog about every topic that interests you. And, yes, this might generate website traffic. Yet, it might not generate the *right traffic* to produce good return-on-investment (ROI).

To avoid the temptation of writing blog articles about too broad a range of topics: vacations, learning to fish, cleaning out your garage, potty training your toddler, moving into a new house, finding great mystery novels, character development, interacting with book clubs, going to the movies with friends, etc., create a blog calendar. And make keyword research your friend. That's because you'll want to add good keywords to your blog articles to pull in search engine traffic. But don't stuff articles with keywords. Your blog articles should read and flow naturally.

Check out this sample blog calendar that covers one month of blog writing:

Date	Topic	Keywords
1/1	Book Characters as Imaginary Partners	Book characters, books with strong female leads, character encyclopedia
1/8	Character Development Techniques	Fully developed character, character development list
1/15	Top 10 Ways to Meet Your Favorite Book Authors (include 3 events you'll appear at)	Books like gone girl, writers meeting, meeting authors
1/22	About Blog Tour Book Giveaways (mention giveaways you're conducting)	Author giveaways, audiobook giveaway, author book giveaways
1/29	Where to Catch Favorite Authors on the Radio (include 1-2 of your radio interviews)	Author radio interviews, online podcasts

It's a good idea to write and publish a new blog article once a week, if not more. Here's a way to avoid feeling pressured to write a new blog article.

Sit down and write one to three months of blog articles over two days. Back up your blog articles, in case you have computer issues. *In fact, regularly back up all of your important files.*

Then, all you have to do is publish the already written articles each week. If you write three months of blog articles at once, you could write new articles every one or two months, keeping yourself ahead of the curve.

Also, link your blog to your official author website. You might be surprised at how much traffic your blog articles pull in. To continue growing your blog traffic, mention your blog during podcast, radio and newsletter interviews. Also, mention your blog if you guest write for newspapers, magazines and other blogs. Simply include the name of your blog in your author byline when you write for media outlets.

Generate more interest in your books with a book blog tour. Following are tips on participating in book blog tours.

Prizes and Giveaways

Book blog tours are becoming increasingly popular. Not only are they effective at building traffic for blog owners, they are effective at introducing readers to new authors. In fact, book blog tours are known for introducing avid book readers to writers who have been writing engaging stories for decades but who, until now, the readers had not heard about.

Book Blogs Surface Bestsellers

And if you absolutely love to read, you probably want to get your hands on the best books. You might even want to be amongst the first people to read new books that go on to become bestsellers worldwide. Book blog tours can help you to do this.

A good way to find book blogs is to check out directories like the Book Blog Directory at http://directory.kaysbookshelf.com. [As a tip, if you own a book blog, you can submit your blog to the directory to gain additional exposure.]

Look for blogs that offer prizes and giveaways. For example, you might be able to win a free ebook reader, discount coupons to retail websites like Barnes & Noble or Amazon.com or you might win a gift card to an offline retailer. While on a blog tour I gave away two free copies of my new book, <u>Love Pour Over Me</u>, at each tour stop.

When you participate in book blog tours, you also might win a free autographed print copy of an author's latest novel or you could win a mug, tote bag or umbrella that has a cool writing quote printed on it. Yes! You absolutely can grab these rewards by simply visiting and participating in book blog tours.

As an author, be the one who's offering free autographed copies of your books. Also, offer other giveaways (e.g. bookmarks, t-shirts). Make sure that your book cover and website URL are on giveaways.

Authors Getting the Most out of Book Blog Tours
Blog tours can include a blend of written and oral author interviews. They can also include book reviews, with some blog tour hosts posting reviews of your books at retail websites like Amazon.com, Google Books or Barnes & Noble.com. During the early days that your book is on the market, these book reviews can be particularly influential, helping book buyers to decide whether or not they want to pay for and read your book.

Then again, for book buyers like me, the reviews might not hold much weight as I decide whether or not to buy and read a book based on excerpts I read. I've got to get a feel for the writer's style, the way the writer works with words, causing them to flow like sweet music. All said -- book reviews certainly don't hurt.

Other rewards and benefits you can receive as an author conducting book blog tours include, of course, introducing yourself and your books to new readers. This is a key takeaway for authors. After all, if you plan on enjoying a lengthy writing career, you want to attract new readers. Blog tours definitely helped me to introduce Raymond Clarke and other main characters in Love Pour Over Me to new readers.

Additional Book Blog Tour Benefits
As an author, whether you write fiction or nonfiction, when you go on blog tours, you can reap benefits. Some of these benefits include:

- Creating relationships with blog owners (make sure that you thank blog owners for supporting you before and after your blog tour runs)

- Opportunities to conduct your first radio interviews
- Reasons to write and distribute press releases about your new books
- Chance to have your name, bio and book information listed at several book blogs
- Additional links tracking to your official author website (this helps to improve your website's search engine rankings)
- Opportunities to answer questions posed by blog visitors

As a tip, when scheduling book blog tours, I recommend that you pay no more than $50 to $60 for a four-week blog tour. I paid $50 for a four-week blog tour which put my book, Love Pour Over Me, in front of thousands of book buyers.

To get the most out of your blog tour, make sure that you create accounts at social media sites like Facebook, Linkedin, Twitter, GoodReads, Mix and Instagram. Share your blog interviews with follows at these social media sites.

If you're on Good Reads, list your blog tour schedule at your Good Reads personal blog and in the Good Reads events section. Invite your Good Reads friends to attend your book blog tour.

Above all – have fun – lots of it! After all, isn't that why you write? Because you love it!

"To reach more readers and take your sales to the next level, you must proactively market your book."
-- Mark Coker

Chapter 7 - Podcasts/Radio Interviews

As of October 2020, there were more than 1,500,000 podcasts.[4] That doesn't even factor the number of episodes that each podcast has. And, people are tuning into podcasts from home, work, their vehicle, the gym, etc.

Comedy is queen when it comes to podcast popularity. More people listened to comedy podcasts as of 2018 than any other podcast type. Education and news podcasts were the next most popular podcast types as of 2018.

Here's another stat that shows the reach of podcasts. 80% of the people who listen to podcasts, tune into a podcast's entire episode. The fact that 65% of the people who listen to podcasts have been listening to podcasts for less than three years, shows how podcast are growing in popularity.

Regarding the devices that people catch podcasts on, smart phones are rising fast, with smart phone podcast usage increasing by as much as 157% since 2014.[4] Here's another plus of marketing your books on podcasts.

People who listen to podcasts are active on social media. They are also more likely to follow a brand that they like on social media. Subjects that podcasts focus on range from education to sports to news, politics, religion, fashion to health and wellness to, of course, books.

Even more, authors who write books on subjects that a podcast is focused on could be viewed as an "expert". These authors might be well received by podcasts hosts and their listeners.

As an author, there are probably hundreds or more podcasts that you could interview on. For example, if you wrote a romance novel, you could interview on podcasts about relationships, creativity, how to keep romance alive or working in the arts.

If you're a self-published romance novelist, you could also interview on podcasts that focus on being an entrepreneur, operating a small business and marketing.

Think big and with an open mind as you create a list of podcasts that you want to interview on. Read the podcasts descriptions to ensure that your book is a fit for the show. Pay attention to:

- Dates and times that the podcasts airs
- Episode length
- Whether or not the show is live or recorded
- Listener demographics (The right podcasts will help you tap into your book's target audience. In other words, if the people who buy your books are single women between the ages of 28 and 40 who have a college degree and earn $60K and up a year, also look for podcasts with this audience demographic.)
- Audience reach (e.g. does the podcast have 1,000 listeners, 10,000 listeners or 1 million listeners per episode)

Another element to check is cost. Some podcasters require their guests to pay a fee to appear on the show. However, there are plenty of podcasters who don't charge a fee.

Consider approaching podcasts interviews with a long term focus. Instead of interviewing on a podcast once, appear on the podcast twice a year. Also, consider interviewing on dozens of podcasts each time you launch a new book.

This is another time when a tool like a spreadsheet is a friend. Check out this sample spreadsheet template that you could use to track podcasts and radio interviews. It's a simple template that you could create in a matter of minutes.

Book Marketing Podcast Schedule						
Podcast Name	Podcast URL	Contact Name	Email	Date Contacted Host to Request Interview	Interview Date	Interview Time

Book focused podcasts that you could interview on include Book Riot, All The Books, Overdue, You're Booked and Off The Shelf Books at https://www.blogtalkradio.com/denise-turney- (*Yours truly hosts this podcast; it's been airing for more than 10 years.*)

Other book podcasts include Ink To Film, Black Chick Lit, The Penguin Podcast, Back Listed, Fresh Air and When In

Romance. But, as has been previously noted, there are hundreds (maybe more, depending on your book's topic) of podcasts that you could interview on.

Check the resources section at the end of this chapter for podcasts directories. But first, more about scheduling podcasts interviews. Keep reading to learn how you could engage hosts and listeners during podcasts interviews. You may hear hosts invite you back more and more. That gives you a chance to deepen your connections with the podcast's listeners.

Also, because podcasts and radio shows are so similar, we're going to cover both in this next section. Conduct a few podcasts interviews then do one to two radio interviews and you'll see how similar the two media forms are.

Using Radio to Sell Books
Radio is another book marketing tool, another way to gain exposure for your titles. However, gaining the most from radio (and podcasts) may take practice.

One difference between podcasts and radio has to do with the equipment used to conduct the shows. For instance, hosts can conduct podcasts episodes using only a laptop, a webcam and a laptop microphone. Landline telephones are said to come across clearer than cell phones when conducting radio or podcast interviews. That applies for both hosts and guests.

Radio DJs use a mixer console, microphone, a headphones distributor, speaker monitors, headphones, microphone arms, an audio processor, transmitter, receiver, antenna and cables. Yet, two of the biggest differences between podcasts and radio is that radio is generally audio only.

You could interview on a podcast that's only audio. Or, you could conduct a podcast interview that uses video and audio. For instance, you might do a podcast interview on Zoom, YouTube or Spreaker. Video podcasts require more equipment for the host than audio only podcasts.

Whether you're conducting an audio only (radio or podcast) interview, you'll generally only focus on answering the interviewers questions. Depending on the show, you also might field questions from listeners.

You can find out if a podcast uses video by reading the show's description. Or you can ask the podcast host if you'll be connecting to the show via video or audio only. For radio, you'll almost always be on audio only, even if you do the interview live inside the actual radio station.

Landing Radio Interviews
The way that you approach podcasts hosts, radio station owners and DJs makes a difference. To schedule radio station interviews, visit the station's website. Get the name of the host or DJ who you want to be interviewed by. When you email the radio station, address your correspondence to this person by name. Highlight your book's benefits, what readers will gain (i.e. new ways to avoid high blood pressure, how to graduate from college without creating student loan debt) from reading your book. It's these details and benefits that you want to focus on during your interview. *Note: Follow this same process when reaching out to podcast hosts to schedule interviews.*

And make it easy for the DJ. For example, you can create a list of 5 to 8 questions for DJs to ask you. In addition to saving DJs' time (trust me, most interviewers will really appreciate this), this step can help the focus of the interview remain on topics that you want to cover. Although there's no guarantee that the DJ will ask questions you send her or him, it doesn't hurt.

Check out these **sample questions** that you could send podcasts hosts and radio station DJs. *Note: Wait until you land the interview to send the questions.*

Sample Radio/Podcast Questions to Send Interviewers
1. Why did you start writing?
2. Tell us the process that you follow to develop characters.
3. What drives your book's main characters?
4. Do you plan on turning the book into a series? Why or why not?
5. Please give us a brief overview of your book.
6. How have book clubs been responding to your book?

During podcasts and radio interviews, expect to introduce yourself. Keep introductions to 1 to 2 minutes. Mention your book titles and your author website URL during the introduction. Following are more steps that you can take to get the most out of radio and podcasts interviews.

Getting the Most Out of Interviews
If this is your first time conducting a radio or podcast interview, practice interviewing with a relative or friend. Relax. Pretend that you're being interviewed by an

actual radio DJ or podcast host. During practice sessions and actual interviews, work to engage listeners. Avoid trying to sell your book and focus on sharing valuable information.

Be natural. Just be wonderful you! Answer questions as if you're having a conversation with the DJ or host. As a tip, stay away from one-word answers. Even if a DJ or host doesn't ask you open ended questions, be conversational. This makes conducting the interview easy for the DJ or host, and they love that!

Also, follow the interviewer's flow. Radio DJs and podcasts hosts have lots of personality. They're generally outgoing, energetic and engaging.

After you land an interview, tell your family, friends, colleagues and book supporters about your interview. Post information (i.e. date, time, location, URL) about your radio interview at social media networks. To get more exposure, create and send a press release about the interview. The more people who tune into your radio interview, the better. Get enough listeners, and you might be asked back.

On the day of the actual interview, arrive 15 to 20 minutes early, 5 to 10 minutes may be enough for podcasts. If you're not certain how early to show up, ask the DJ or podcast host. Dress comfortably but professionally. Again, relax. Have fun.

If you're doing a television interview or video podcast, check your hair, etc. Most podcast video shows capture your chest and above. Television stations may capture your entire body. For video podcast, make sure that you're in a room with a background that presents well.

Here's another tip. When doing video interviews at night or when outside light is low, place a lamp on a desk so that the light is facing you. This may keep you from looking blurry on the screen. Lighting really is a big deal when it comes to video or television.

Podcasts and Radio Resources
To help you even more as you start scheduling radio and podcasts interviews, I've researched and pulled together a list of resources. These resources should save you time and effort.

Podcasts Directories / Lists

Save yourself time of searching for podcasts to interview on. Look through podcasts directories and lists instead of searching the Internet for book focused podcasts one by one.

- **Oprah Recommended Book Podcasts -** https://www.oprahmag.com/entertainment/books/g29194023/best-book-podcasts/
- **Apple (This is a top directory, maybe #1) -** https://podcasts.apple.com/us/genre/podcasts/id26
- **Spotify** - https://open.spotify.com/genre/podcasts-page
- **Google Podcasts -** https://play.google.com/store/apps/details?id=com.google.android.apps.podcasts&hl=en_US&gl=US
- **Blog Talk Radio** - https://www.blogtalkradio.com/
- **Artists Network -** https://www.artistsnetwork.com/artist-life/12-art-podcasts-inspiration/
- **Buzzsprout -** https://www.buzzsprout.com/learn/podcast-directory
- **Medium** - https://medium.com/swlh/the-29-best-self-publishing-podcast-episodes-of-all-time-2bb449790fb8
- **RSS Feed** - https://rss.com/blog/podcast-directory-list/ (if you start your own literary or books podcast, this is a good list to add that podcast to in order to grow traffic)

Radio Directories / Lists

- **Live 365** - https://live365.com/blog/online-radio-directories/
- **Radio Locator** - https://radio-locator.com/
- **Cloud Rad** - https://www.cloudrad.io/internet-radio-directory/
- **NPR Radio Stations** - https://legacy.npr.org/stations/pdf/nprstations.pdf

While reaching out to DJs to schedule radio interviews, consider contacting your local radio stations. Go for local radio stations that have talk shows.

As a tip, most radio stations interview guests. Even radio stations that almost solely play music, conduct guest interviews. Highlight how their listeners will benefit from information that you share during interviews.

"You think someone else should do the marketing? It would be nice if it worked that way, but it doesn't."
-- Sensible Solutions

Chapter 8 - Online Book Marketing

Throughout this chapter, we will focus on tools, websites and resources that you can access to market your books online. But, before we start, it's important to note that there are many ways to sell books offline too. In fact, you could sell books in offline non-bookstore markets. More about that later in <u>Book Marketing That Drives Up Book Sales</u>.

Regarding online book marketing, in addition to marketing your books via radio, digital television and podcast interviews and online book and blog tours, let's start exploring places to sell your print, digital and audio books. Of course, the giant online bookseller is Amazon.com.

Kobo, Google Books, Cushcity, Mahogany Books, Books A Million, Barnes & Noble, Powell's Books, Apple Books, Okada Books, Half Price Books Canada, Audible, Alibris, Better World Books, Valore and Indigo are other online booksellers that you may want to offer your books for sale at. If your book is published through a traditional publisher, your publisher should set your book up with online and offline book retailers.

As a self-published author, you can work with the company (e.g. Smashwords, Ebookit) that you publish your book through. These companies can add your books to distributor and book retailer systems for you.

Of course, you could reach out to book retailers yourself and request that they add your book to their platforms. However, this could take a lot of time. That's why it's recommended that you work through the company that publishes or prints your books.

But don't just get your book added to online bookseller websites. Set up your author profile at each of these bookseller websites.

For example, features to add to your Amazon author page include:

- Setting up your Amazon Author Central Page
- Compelling descriptions to your books. Include relevant keywords in the descriptions. But make sure that the writing flows and is not jagged or stuffed with keywords.

- Link from your official author website blog
- Professional author photo
- Videos of you at book events
- Podcasts and radio interview videos, etc.
- Strong author bio

If you've published three or more books, consider creating an Amazon store to attract more readers. You set up Amazon stores through the Amazon Advantage portal.

Should you publish your book through Amazon Kindle Direct Publishing (KDP), run giveaways. Also, try price promotions and countdowns. For both price promotions and countdowns, you'll lower the price of your book over a certain period.

Get more out of countdowns and price deals by running ads in free and discounted eBook directories.

Also, nominate your KDP select book to be included in Kindle Deals and for Prime Reading. Simply click the "Marketing" link at the top of the Kindle Direct Publishing site to nominate your book for these marketing services. Here's another tip, if you do publish through KDP, consider choosing expanded distribution for your print books.

With KDP Select, you'll only be able to sell your eBook through Amazon. You may not even be able to sell your eBook direct at your website, unless it links to Amazon for purchase.

However, if you go with Amazon print expanded distribution, you can sell your print book through libraries, brick and mortar bookstores and non-bookstore outlets.

Setting Up Your Amazon Author Page
Let's walk through setting up your Amazon author page.

- Set up an Amazon Author Central (https://author.amazon.com/home) account if you don't already have one. Next:
- Click "Profile" at the top of the page
- Add a strong bio. Include SEO keywords in your bio to support attracting search engine traffic
- Click "Blog Updates" to link your official author website blog to your Amazon Author Central page
- Go to "Upload Photos" to upload a professional photo

- Add pictures of your books (e.g. pictures of you or readers holding your books, a heavily trafficked book signing event)
- Click the "Books" link to add your books to your profile
- Preview your author's page by clicking "Go" below "Author Page". Preview the page and make changes as needed

Under the "Reports & Marketing" tab at the top of your Author Central page, you can check the ranking for your books. Also, concerning your book's ranking, take your time choosing the categories that you'll use for your books when you set them up for sale at Amazon. Note: Traditional publishers may automatically handle this for you. Non-traditional eBook publishers, will ask you which categories you want to sale your books under at Amazon.

You can select up to three categories. I encourage you to use all three. Go for categories that are related to your book but that are *niche categories*. This helps your book to rank higher in these less used book categories.

Setting up an Amazon Advantage Store
To set up an Amazon Store, create an Amazon Advantage account (https://advantage.amazon.com/advantage/home).

- After your account is setup, log into Amazon Advantage and click "Advertising".
- Then, click "Manage Campaigns". On the left side of the page, there's a three-line menu icon. Click that. Next, click "Stores" and "Create Store".
- Follow the prompts. You can also use the Store Builder tool to create your Amazon Store. It may be best to wait until you have three or more books before you set up a store.

Amazon will approve your store before it's live. After your store is created and approved, use the URL to advertise your books for sale at Amazon on social media.

Also, continue to advertise your official author website. The Amazon Store simply gives book buyers another way to find and purchase your titles. Sharing your Amazon Store URL also gives you a way to showcase all of your books in one place, without having to send social media, etc. posts for each of your books.

Using Social Media To Market Books

Social media is effective for book marketing because social media puts you in contact with potentially thousands or millions of book buyers, at the click of a button. Nearly 50% of the world's population uses social media. That's over 3 billion users worldwide.[11] According to Statista, Facebook is the most popular social media app, with 169.76 million monthly mobile users as of September 2019.[5]

Instagram was next. It was followed by Facebook Messenger, Twitter, Pinterest, Reddit and Snapchat. About 45.98 million United States users accessed the Snapchat mobile app as of September 2019.[5]

That's a lot of users, for sure. However, don't go into social media book marketing thinking that you'll reach millions of people just because you keep posting images, videos and print ads of your books.

In fact, you might only reach 10% of the people in your Facebook stream. The same applies to posting book ads in Facebook groups. A small number of group members might see your ads. Even more, it's not uncommon for authors to, unknowingly, posts book ads to other authors in Facebook groups who are also posting one book ad after another, neither author ever intending to buy the other's book.

Here's what Facebook has to say about posts in response to a Facebook group admin question. "If your **group** has fewer than 250 **people**, **posts** will be marked as Seen **after** they're read. If your **group** reaches 250 members or more, you'll no longer **see** who's seen **posts**. For **posts** that have been seen: Seen by [Number] will appear next to each **post** to indicate how **many group** members have seen it."[6]

I'm an admin for two Facebook groups. For the private, niche group with 191 members, about 7 people may see a post. Someone adds a new post to the group 1 to 2 times a week. In more active groups, posts might be seen by more people. Even so, the above can give you an idea of the percentage of people who might see a Facebook group post.

Yet, although *everyone* (or even half the people on the group) may never see your post, that doesn't mean that Facebook, Twitter, Pinterest, Snapchat, LinkedIn, etc. aren't effective tools to use to introduce your books to readers. In fact, AdExpresso shares that, "There are 1.82 billion daily active users on Facebook, as of 2020, and over 2.7 billion monthly active users."[7]

As previously shared, not all of these users are engaged on the platform. For example, AdExpresso also reports that, "Facebook users made an average of 5 comments, 12 post likes, 1 share and 1 page like in October 2020."[7]

This was during a contentious United States presidential election. The numbers could be lower during a non-election year. Here's another statistic to consider when marketing books on Facebook or another social media platform.

"The average engagement rate for Pages with fewer than 10,000 fans is about .52%, but as you gain more fans, the average decreases."[7] Next, let's explore Twitter and take a look at how much reach a single tweet might have.

Jack Dorsey, Twitter's founder, sent the first tweet on the platform on March 21, 2006. As of 2019, there were 330 million active Twitter users, according to Brandwatch.[8] About 145 million users are on Twitter each day.

"Based on US accounts, 10% of users write 80% of tweets."[8] 79% of Twitter accounts are outside of the United States. And, of all active users, 80% access Twitter via a mobile device. This is another reason to have a mobile friendly author website. Add a link to a tweet that directs users to your website and a mobile friendly author website that downloads fast could keep those people exploring your website for 30 seconds or longer.

Exploring Social Media Platforms

Tik Tok had 800 million active users as of 2020. It was the most downloaded app in the Apple IOS store during the first quarter of 2019. Additionally, 41% of Tik Tok users are between 16 and 24 years old.[9] (*Does this fit your book's demographic?*)

What about Instagram? This is what Buffer shares, "The reality is that people usually don't see all the new posts when they visit Instagram." Furthermore, "A study by Instagram themselves found that before the algorithm, on average, users missed 70 percent of the posts on their feeds and 50 percent of the posts from their friends. Now, though, Instagram's 800 million users reportedly see 90 percent of their friends' posts."[10]

This might help you to know what to do to get more eyes on your book marketing posts. "As long as you are creating engaging, relevant, and timely content, the algorithm is actually an advantage to you. It will help to surface your great content to more of your followers than when posts were arranged reverse-chronologically."[10]

Also, social media accounts (and some website traffic) comes from bots. In other words, actual people aren't making all the posts, Likes, tweets or views. Instead, computerized software programs (bots) are creating a lot of noise on social media platforms and websites.

One final stat that's important as you consider how you will reach your target audience. "In 2019, 90.4% of Millennials, 77.5% of Generation X, and 48.2% of Baby Boomers were active social media users."[11]

Now, that you have a better view of the numbers of users on leading social media platforms, let's look at actions that you could take to find and engage book buyers.

Ways to Connect with Social Media Book Buyers
Video is growing in popularity. Another popular social media feature is an image. Furthermore, hashtags (#) are used on Twitter, Facebook, LinkedIn and Instagram to highlight the subject of a post. Examples of this include:

- #Mysterybook lovers are falling hard for this new #thriller
- Stuck in the house? Nothing beats boredom better than #reading a good #book
- Find out the truth about Keisha and Tyrone's #relationship in It Started With Love, the new hit #romancenovel

So, use hashtags when posting to social media platforms that use hashtags. Another tip is to use trending hashtags in the body of your social media posts. Just make sure that the trending hashtags are relevant to your book.

Here's a list of more ways to find, connect with and engage book buyers on social media:

- Post free book excerpts on social media, being sure to include links to your author website or book order pages.
- Announce dates, locations (i.e. street address, website URL) and times for upcoming author interviews on social media. For example, if you're interviewing on online radio shows like Off The Shelf, post flyers about the interviews on social media.

- Share pictures of book covers on Pinterest. Again, to get the most out of the posts, it's important to include links to your author website or book order pages.
- Publish links to book blog posts on social media.
- Support other authors and book readers on social media by commenting on interesting posts.
- Create a strong social media profile. Do for each social media account that you have.
- Add quotes about book characters to social media updates.
- Alert social media users to book giveaways that you're running.
- Post images and book mockups of your discounted books. Post how much of a discount you're running on the book.
- Share links to your live book interviews and your live book readings
- Send out the link to your latest literary newsletter.
- Offer a free chapter of your latest book. Or offer a free chapter of one of your backlist (older) books.
- Run a social media contest. Give the winner a coupon, gift card or a free copy of your latest book.

How To Design Low Cost Social Media Visuals

Social media book marketing can do one of two things. Go down the road of social media book marketing and you could spend loads of time (I'm talking hours every week) only to yield small results. This is a path of frustration and disillusion. I know. I've been on this road before.

You could also find a way to tap into the right active social media book audience. Connect these book lovers to an effective message and watch your book sales increase. Visuals, especially when combined with clear audio, are great ways to marry the right message with the right audience.

Smart Book Marketing Design Tools

Here are design platforms that can save you time. These design tools are intuitive. You can figure out how to use them in as little as a few minutes. Even more, pricing on these design programs are inexpensive. I've used more than one of the below tools to design book marketing visuals in less than 10 minutes. Because I generally reuse book marketing designs that I create, after I create the designs, I save them as a PDF or JPEG.

That way, I can publish the book marketing designs to several social media platforms. It's also a cool way to keep social media book marketing messaging fresh. As a tip, include your website URL (or the URL to the site that you want book readers to click on and visit) on the design. And now, to the low cost book marketing design platforms:

- Affinity - https://affinity.serif.com/en-us/: Affinity Publisher works with iPad, Mac and Windows. Book marketing visuals that you can create with Affinity rival top professional marketing designs. The Windows version cost $49.99. Images are crisp, sharp, definitely attention grabbing.
- Book Brush - https://bookbrush.com/: Book Brush offers free and paying book design services. You can build book mockups (i.e. an image of a woman holding your book), book covers, banners and social media posts and ads using Book Brush. Their paid services come with more mockups templates and an unlimited number of downloads. They also offer free webinars to show you how to create engaging social media book designs. BookBrush's Plus Plan is $99 annually (but doesn't include expanded MockUps). Their Gold Plan is $146 a year and their Platinum

Plan is $246 a year). They run plan discounts. So, keep your eyes open for those.

- Bootstrap - https://getbootstrap.com/: Blog headers, one page websites, book marketing visual carousels and analytics are a few design options at Bootstrap. Similar to Canva, Bootstrap offers themes that you can use to kick off new book marketing designs. You have to install the program to use it.
- Canva – https://www.canva.com/: I love Canva because of how easy it is to use. There's the option to select book marketing designs like book covers, posters, postcards and social media posts. You can use existing designs, plop in your own images or edit Canva templates. There are free designs and low cost designs. Another feature that I love about Canva is there print options. I use this to create postcards that I snail mail to media, book clubs, etc.
- Constant Contact – https://www.constantcontact.com: Although I don't consider Constant Contact to be a true book marketing design platform, Constant Contact does have templates that you can use to create newsletters and presentations that you can push out to target book buyers. Cost depends on the size of your mailing list but can be as low as $39.99 a month. Recommend using Constant Contact (or a

similar program) if you plan to automate and maintain a contact list.

- Fixma - https://www.figma.com: Pricing for Fixma starts at "Free" and works up to $45 a month. Pricing depends on the number of editors working on your designs.
- Keynote - https://www.apple.com/keynote/: This application uses the Cloud to let you design and edit presentations.
- Pixelmator - https://www.pixelmator.com: Great design tool to build out book marketing visuals, especially if you have design experience. You can buy a package for as little as $39.99.

Marketing and selling books is ongoing, persistent work. It's not for the faint of heart. It takes vision, passion, commitment and drive. You have to make the right choices often enough to scale. The above book marketing design tools could help you to deliver effective messaging about your books to the right book buyers.

Save Time With Social Media Schedulers
Social media scheduling tools like Buffer, Hootsuite, Vistaprint Digital Marketing, Sendible, SocialBee and SEMrush can save you hours. Prices for these social

media scheduling tools range from less than $10 a month to $29 a month to $99.95 a month.[12]

Working with a team of marketers to sell your book? Look for a scheduling tool that allows 3 or more people to post to social media platforms from your account. Other features to consider include:

- Schedule videos, images and written posts (e.g. quotes, news articles) individually or in bulk, potentially covering a week or a month of posts.
- Access the publisher calendar to schedule posts at certain hours / days of the week.
- Select social media platforms to publish different types of posts to.
- Assign content to be approved by your or your book marketing manager.
- Identify posts that are getting the most Likes, Shares and Comments. Reschedule these posts to gain more traction.
- Add a Chrome extension to add posts to your social media scheduling tool while you're surfing the web.
- Categorize posts (e.g. book quotes, book reviews, discounts)

Prepare to invest three to four hours (or more) during one day on social media scheduling. During a single day, you could schedule enough posts to cover three to four months in this amount of time. Mix it up. For instance, schedule:

- Video on Monday
- Newsletter on Tuesday
- Picture of you signing your books on Wednesday
- Motivational quote on Thursday
- Details of a book price discount on Friday
- Picture of you riding a bike on Saturday (include a funny quote and your website URL with the post)
- Short excerpt from your latest book on Sunday

Also, post at least one book ad (using tools like book mockups, backgrounds and animation) each day. And, in addition to using automated scheduling tools, log onto social media platforms and post questions, comments, Likes, etc. in *real time*.

Book Marketing Platforms That Work
You can get real traction on the right book marketing platforms using two marking strategies. One approach requires more of your time. The other approach requires more money.

Types of Book Marketing Platforms

AALBC.com, Book Daily, Artist First and Good Reads are types of book marketing platforms. So too are TED Talk, Mosaic, podcasts and social media.

Book clubs, television programs that focus on books, press release distribution services and bookstores are also types of book marketing platforms. But it's your book blog and author website that are your primary platforms.

Each platform that you work should point back to either your author website or your book order page. If your only book order page is at Amazon.com or BarnesandNoble.com, point platforms to your custom sales pages at those bookseller websites.

Getting Platforms Results

That means that your social media profiles should include the link to either your author website or book order page. When you run ads through marketing agencies like Book Daily, add a link to your book order page in your profile.

If you have the time, schedule at least an hour a day to work book marketing platforms. The more time you invest at the platforms, the better. But don't just posts. Find out who platform influencers are. Ask influencers questions. Also, "like" what they share and follow them.

I'm a fan of social media posts schedulers. Just log into social media accounts and posts *live* once a day. You can get results with 10 to 15 minutes of work per social media platform.

Working Book Marketing Platforms
Pick two to three social media platforms to actively posts comments, ask questions and share motivational quotes on. See if your followers, shares, likes and overall engagement don't go up.

Build your book marketing platforms by:

- Blogging once a week or more (add keywords into your blog posts)
- Sending direct mail to book lovers
- Creating and distributing a weekly or a monthly newsletter

- Scheduling at least one YouTube, Vimeo, etc. video posts or a Roku television, etc. posts a week
- Guest posting on high traffic websites like *Huffington Post, Guardian Books, Essence, Forbes* and *Entrepreneur*. Include a link to your author website in your bio.
- Attending large book club events and cultural festivals. Pass out free bookmarks or book excerpts. Stamp your author website URL on all handouts.

Take two to three of the above steps at least once a week. If you're short on time, consider paying experienced, reputable book marketing agencies to do your heavy lifting. Start small with spending. Avoid giving into smooth sales pitches and getting pulled into expensive book marketing deals.

Measure Results

Make sure that you see measurable results, and not just an increase in traffic. Why is this important? Computer bots can send loads of traffic your way, lending the appearance that lots of people are truly interested in your book, when that's not the case.

Additionally, don't assume that just because your profile, website URL or book cover is at book marketing platforms that you're pulling in the *right traffic*. An increase in book sales is a sure sign that book marketing platforms are working.

Requests for book excerpts, author interviews, more social media followers and increased reader engagement are other signs that book marketing platforms are yielding good results. If you receive more comments that focus on your book or its topics at your book blog after launching a book marketing campaign, it could be an additional indicator that platforms you're on are pulling in your target audience.

"The worth of a book is to be measured by what you can carry away from it." -- James Bryce

Chapter 9 - Book Reviews

Book reviews are valuable book marketing tools for several reasons. Some readers only buy books that have five or more reviews. And there are book marketing websites that won't run ads for books that have no reviews.

You'll find books that get 99% positive reviews. Other books receive a mix of reviews. Write a good book and you should have an overall review of 3 out of 5 stars or higher. This represents the *average* of all of the reviews that you received.

Amazon used to limit the reviews that it posts to reviews from verified book buyers. Since Amazon bought GoodReads in 2013, I've noticed that GoodReads reviews for books are pulling into the overall rating on Amazon. Sounds great, except that, as of the first printing of Book Marketing That Drives Up Book Sales, GoodReads does not verify that its members actually purchased a book before they post a review rating.

However, joining GoodReads discussion forums and participating in the forums to build relationships with readers is a good way to start reaching out for book reviews. For instance, after you've been participating on a GoodReads discussion forum or group for a month, submit a post asking members to review your book.

Tie the request in with a discount or free book countdown that you're running. Also, encourage colleagues, family and friends who purchase your book to leave a review.

In fact, whenever you know the person who bought your book, ask them to post a review on at least one book retailer website. To get book reviews, also:

- Send ARCs to book reviewers and book columnists. Ask them to review your book and send you the review.
- Contact book bloggers, requesting a review (be prepared to send them a free copy of your book)
- Submit your book to book review websites. Just make sure that you work with reputable book review companies.

- Keep marketing your book. The more sales that your book gets, the more reviews the book should receive.

After you start receiving book reviews, use those reviews to market your book. Here are ways to use reviews to market and sell more books:

- Include a review from an influencer or a household named author on your book's front cover.
- Add book reviews to your official author website.
- Post quality book reviews on your social media platforms. Include images and/or video with the reviews for impact.
- Incorporate book reviews in marketing materials (e.g. direct email, newsletters, postcards, flyers).
- Mention good book reviews during podcasts, newspaper, magazine, blog, television and radio interviews.
- Put good book reviews in press releases.

"There are only seven days in a week, and someday isn't one of them." -- Anonymous

Chapter 10 - Literary Newsletters

Social media rose to prominence and it was as if email, particularly email newsletters, went out the window in the eyes of some authors. Yet, it's newsletter subscriber contact information that authors can call their own, not followers at large social media networks. That information is owned by shareholders and/or company founders.

Online Newsletters Increase Customer Engagement
The more media outlets that you are on as an author, the more leverage you may have to make changes to your marketing strategy. For example, if you grow your literary newsletter subscriber base from 1,000 to 30,000 a month, you have direct access to those subscribers.

And, you may not have to pay to promote social media posts to reach large numbers of supporters. Instead, you can simply publish sales and book discount details in your monthly newsletter. You can also email holiday greetings to your literary newsletter subscribers.

To save time building a literary newsletter, consider using software. Companies that offer newsletter software and a broad range of newsletter layouts include Constant Contact, Vertical Response, Mail Chimp and iContact. Using intuitive templates, it's possible to design a newsletter in less than an hour.

Build Engaging Email Newsletters
Fields that you generally can complete while building an online newsletter are:

- Your name or your publishing company name
- A company logo (it's good to give subscribers an image that they can easily recall; consider using the same logo you use at your website, on media kits, etc.)
- Letter from the editor (personal notes, words of encouragement, tidbits about recent learning experiences or successes that you've had are good items to share)
- Pictures of recent book signings that you attended, hosted or sponsored
- Discount coupons that loyal subscribers can use to enjoy additional savings on your books
- Feature author interviews

- Paid writing jobs
- Writing quotes
- Book excerpts
- List of upcoming events, contests, etc. that your subscribers will benefit from knowing about

Tips to Grow Online Newsletter Subscriber Base
As with other marketing strategies that you implement, measure the return on your investment (ROI). As a tip, newsletter software companies generally deliver metrics on each newsletter that you distribute. The metrics may be sent within 48 or 72 hours of the date you distribute a weekly or monthly newsletter.

Review newsletter metrics. They can reveal changes you that you need to make to improve subscriber engagement, so that you can increase the numbers of clicks, new subscribers and social media shares that you get with each issue. When choosing newsletter software companies, also consider looking for companies that give you the option to add social media share buttons to newsletters. One other tip, consider adding subscription buttons for your newsletter to your website and blog so that you can grow your readership.

*"It's never too early to start marketing your book." --
Heather Hart*

Chapter 11 - Build Your Own Contact List

Don't be fooled by social media. You need your own electronic subscriber contact list. With tools like Excel, Word and Outlook, it's free to create a subscriber contact list. But, that approach is time consuming. You have to add and remove contacts manually.

Going Electronic Gives You Time to Focus on Other Growth Initiatives

Sure. It only takes minutes to keep a small subscriber list updated. When I started The Book Lover's Haven (https://www.chistell.com/newsletter.html) newsletter subscriber contact list, I used Word. Then, I moved to Excel to save time.

My subscriber list grew to the point where it was taking me more than an hour to update the list. At first, I pushed updates out from weekly to monthly. The list kept growing and became more laborious to maintain. Today, I use Constant Contact and let subscribers sign up to receive The Book Lover's Haven themselves. It takes seconds.

If you do use a third party subscriber contact tool (i.e. Emma, Benchmark, Moosend, MailJet, Mail Chimp), consider downloading the list once a month or once a quarter, depending on how fast your list changes. Also, make sure that you only add people to your subscriber contact list who requested to be added.

Benefits of Owning a Subscriber Contact List
Besides giving you control of your contacts, having your own subscriber list puts you in the driver seat. You don't have to follow rules set by social media platform owners. You don't have to compete with other social media users. You can determine the best days and times to send electronic mail to contacts. Other benefits of creating your own subscriber contact list include:

- Opportunities to request contacts' home addresses, so that you can send them printed brochures, catalogs and longer forms of direct mail
- Send contacts custom designed greeting cards
- Mail contacts seasonal or birthday gifts
- Ship coupon books to subscribers
- Add telephone numbers to contact lists, so that you can telephone contacts and sing "Happy Birthday" to

them or to let them know about a great sale that you're running, etc.

- Maintain a way to communicate with supporters if social media platforms shut down
- Eliminate the guesswork out of whether or not you actually reached a real person. Place security features on your subscriber list, and you could keep bots from adding subscribers to your list, lending the false impression that more people are interested in your newsletter than there actually are

Who knows if a social media platform will shut down. If it does and you don't have your own contact list, you can wave good-bye to those contacts.

Relationships that you have built are too valuable to leave to chance. Create your own electronic subscriber contact list and allow supporters to grow and evolve with you, regardless of what's going on in the social media world.

"With your book or your business, you absolutely must know who you're selling to, or else you won't get anywhere." -- Kristen Eckstein

Chapter 12 - Book Club Connections

Book club meetings are events that are rooted in the desire to share an arts passion. Picture it. Chairs circling a living room, library conference room or community center floor. Salad, sweet tea, water and sandwiches line a kitchen counter or a long serving table.

Women, men, or a mix of both genders, sit in folding chairs, books resting atop their laps, smiles lighting their faces. Each person is eager to share his reflections, perspectives and emotions that are related to the book club's latest chosen novel or nonfiction book.

It's like being amid friends. Some opinions about the book are hard, members refusing to shift their perception, despite hearing the voices of other members who share equally passionate views that are opposite their own.

Conversations may become tense. But they never erupt into argument. This is the book club world.

Fortunately, it's into this literary, academic, entertaining and satisfying world that you can enter, and, not only as an avid book reader but now, also as an author. In fact, have your book accepted as a book-of-the-month by a large book club and you could receive hundreds of book sales in a matter of days.

Celebrities and athletes like Oprah Winfrey, Andrew Luck and Reese Witherspoon operate book clubs. Social media influencers, major publishing houses and local book lovers also start and manage book clubs.

There are book clubs that are based on genre. For example, there are romance, mystery and science fiction book clubs. Among the larger book clubs, there's:

- Oprah's Book Club - According to AARP, "Oprah Winfrey's book club is arguably America's most influential literary hit-maker, turning unknown titles into massive best sellers — from its early days on *The Oprah Winfrey Show* to its rebirth in 2012 in the pages of her magazine as "Oprah's Book Club 2.0."[14]
- Reese Witherspoon's Book Club - About this book club, AARP shares, "Each book centers around a woman's story, such as *Untamed,* by Glennon Doyle, a memoir and rallying cry for confident, strong

women; and *The Henna Artist,* by Alka Joshi, a debut novel about an Indian woman's journey after escaping an abusive marriage."[14]

- Andrew Luck Book Club - "The former NFL quarterback started the book club in 2016. The book club "offers a huge range of titles, some of them classics, others just his own quirky favorites."[14]
- Now Read This - A PBS News Hour / *New York Times* book club
- Well Read Black Girl
- The Latina Book Club
- Books & Boba
- The History Book Club
- Goodreads Choice Awards Book Club
- Mystery Book Club
- Science Fiction Book Club

And these are just a few of the many book clubs. In fact, there are hundreds of book clubs, if not more. As you continue your book marketing efforts, reach out to book clubs that read the types of books that you write.

That shared, it's important to note that some book clubs read a broad range of books, taking on romance, family sagas, mysteries, thrillers, science fiction and nonfiction.

Therefore, before you reach out to book club president's, review the book club's description. Also, check out the last five to six books that the club selected as its book-of-the-month.

Email each book club president individually, preferably addressing each president by name. And focus on the benefits (e.g. inspiration, fantasy, stirred romantic emotions, suspense and a desire to figure out who-done-it) that the book club members will gain from reading your book.

Before you reach out to book club presidents, consider participating in book club social media discussions. For instance, you could follow book clubs on Twitter, Facebook or Instagram that you want to select your book to read.

Ask questions about other books that the club is reading. And, post comments. Even more, read one or more of the books that the club selects and actively engage in discussions about that book. In addition to being fun, that engagement could serve as a "soft introduction", connecting you to the clubs' presidents and members.

Here's a sample book club request email / letter that you could send. Save time and copy paste the message, personalizing the email to fit each specific book club that you contact.

SAMPLE LETTER

Dear [Book Club President]:

Thank you for supporting books and literacy. [*Book Title*], [*Book Title*] and [*Book Title*], recent books that your club read are great stories. My book Long Walk Up also offers entertainment, inspiration and mystery depth that your members may readily appreciate.

Mulukan is a powerful woman whose strength is rooted in a rocky childhood. Few would imagine that this girl, orphaned at six-years-old, would become Africa's first woman president. As surprising as the events of Mulukan's life are, readers connect with the story, feel Mulukan's strength, her resolve.

I've included a short three page Long Walk Up excerpt. At your request, I'm happy to send you an ARC for the book. Long Walk Up is a short, powerful read, filling up 110 pages. Please read the excerpt and see if you aren't moved by Mulukan's story.

Please let me know how I can further support your book club.

Thank you again for supporting books and literacy.

With Appreciation,

Denise Turney
Author - Long Walk Up
www.chistell.com

To help you get started as you work to build book club relationships, I've included several book club directories. As a tip, to deepen book club relationships, consider sending book club presidents holiday greetings. For example, you could send book club presidents a printed holiday postcard or an electronic New Year's, Thanksgiving and Christmas postcard.

Book Clubs and Book Club Directories
- Readers Circle - http://www.readerscircle.org/
- Read Divas Read - http://www.realdivasread.com/419013381
- IPL - https://www.ipl.org/div/pf/entry/48523
- AALBC - https://aalbc.com/bookclubs/
- Big Library Read - https://biglibraryread.com/

- Girly Book Club - https://thegirlybookclub.com/
- International House - https://www.ihclt.org/get-involved/book-club/
- Silent Book Club - https://silentbook.club/
- I Love Libraries - http://www.ilovelibraries.org/booklovers/bookclub/find-book-club
- Library Technology - https://librarytechnology.org/libraries/
- Global Library Directory - http://www.librarydir.org/
- American Library Directory - http://www.americanlibrarydirectory.com/
- U.S. Public Libraries - https://librarytechnology.org/libraries/uspublic/

Libraries are included because many book clubs meet at libraries. Another good place to find book clubs is at "Meet Up" (https://www.meetup.com/topics/library/).

Thanks to technology like Zoom and Skype, you might be asked to join a book club meeting virtually. Or you might receive an invitation to appear at a book club in person.

Because you may not know the book club members, attend daytime book club meetings in a public place (e.g. restaurant, library). Relax. Be yourself. You know your book best. So, you should be more than ready to handle Q&A. Be engaging. Help make the meeting fun, entertaining and informative.

"There's no such thing as 'no market'. Some books are just niche oriented, that's all." -- Jo Linsdell

Chapter 13 - Choosing Book Distributors

Book distributors and book wholesalers can get your books into bookstores. The percentage that they keep on each sold book is around 55% to 60%. Distributors aren't cheap. But they do help with bookstore sales.

Ingram is one of the largest book distributors in the world. More than 7 million titles are part of the Ingram system. Baker & Taylor is a distributor that is a leader in getting books into libraries. The distributor's parent company, Follett, "serves more than 90,000 schools and school libraries in the U.S., Canada, and 140 countries," according to the American Booksellers Association.[15]

If you're new to the book industry, get to know how book distributors and wholesalers work. To give you an easy background on distributors and wholesalers, here are quick facts about working with book distributors and book wholesalers:

Ingram and Baker & Taylor work as wholesale distributors. Ingram fulfills orders from book retailers and libraries. As of 2019, Baker & Taylor dropped the retail part of its business and focuses more on fulfilling library orders. In other words, as librarians and individual book buyers purpose your book from a library or from a brick and mortar bookstore, distributors receive the orders, reach out to you or your publisher and get the books to librarians and booksellers. You could work with wholesalers even if you only sell 2 to 10 copies of your books to libraries and bookstores.

This process is a huge time saver. All you have to do is to create an account with a distributor. If you don't work through a distributor, you'd have to create an individual account with each bookstore and library that you wanted to sell books through.

Furthermore, trade distributors place large orders with libraries and bookstores. For instance, a trade distributor might order 3,000 to 6,000 copies of a book.

Another way to get books into bookstores (and non-bookstore locations) is to enter a consignment agreement with a retailer. You may be able to keep a larger percentage of the money earned from the sale of your book. However, a consignment may be with a small, local bookstore. Therefore, unless you market and promote books for sale through the store, you may not sell many copies of your books. Yet, more readers could see and learn about your titles.

Shipping and handling of books to wholesalers and distributors is generally on the traditional publisher or you, if you self-published. Whichever option you choose, be aware that there could be returns.

So, manage your budget wisely. Books that you sell on January 5 could be returned from the bookstore to the distributor back to you on March 30, if the books don't sell.

Here's a list of book distributors and wholesalers, some which accept fiction and nonfiction books:

- https://nonfictionauthorsassociation.com/list-of-book-distributors-and-wholesalers/

As a self-publisher, there's a strong likelihood that you'll publish your book, even if it's only the digital version of your book, through an eBook publisher. IngramSpark, Barnes & Noble Press, Ebookit, Smashwords, Kindle Direct Publishing, iBooks and Kobo are some eBook publishers that you could publish your eBook through.

These eBook publishers can submit your book to online distributors, with one exception. Publish your book through Kindle Direct, and you can also sell your eBook through Amazon. However, Kindle Direct makes it easy for you to sell your books via Amazon's regional markets (e.g. UK, Japan, Canada).

Research eBook publishers before you launch your eBook. Following are insights on features to look from eBook publishers.

How to Choose the Right eBook Publishing Company
Technological products like computers, mobile devices and e-book readers make it possible for book buyers to download and start reading novels and nonfiction books with the click of a button. This convenience has seen e-book sales rise by as much as 117 percent for 2011 according to *Publisher's Weekly*. It's a growing market that authors and people with a story to share may want to get into. After all, publishing e-books can allow writers to receive benefits like royalties, media interview requests and fans. However, not all e-book publishing companies offer the same benefits, some e-book publishing companies even charge higher formatting costs than others.

Yet, there are strong upsides. In fact, publishing e-books can turn you into a bestselling author within a matter of months.

Read Reviews

Search for e-book publishing company reviews and ranking reports. While reading reviews and ranking reports consider factors such as how long the company has been in business, the number of books the company publishes each year and the types of files (e.g. pdf, Word) that the publisher accepts from authors to convert into e-book format.

Ask Published Authors

Contact authors who have already had digital books published and ask them for e-book publishing company recommendations. For example, you can email authors, tell them that you are considering publishing an e-book and ask them to tell you who they think are the top three e-book publishers to work with. Let authors know if your book has illustrations and/or charts and graphs as some e-book publishers may be more experienced at formatting books with illustrations, charts or graphs than others.

Distribution

Ask the e-book publisher for a list of resellers they distribute books to. Types of resellers include Amazon.com, Google Books, Ingram Books, Apple Books, and Barnes & Noble.com. Also find out if e-book publishers have distribution contracts with companies that service libraries as, generally, the more distribution channels a publisher has the more books you may sell. For example, Portia, a classic book about an African American defense attorney dealing with breast cancer, is available to libraries through distributors like Baker & Taylor.

E-Book Readers

Find out the different types of e-book readers the publishing company formats e-books to be read on. Kindle, Nook and Kobo are types of e-book readers. Also check to see if your e-book will be formatted and for sale in portable document format (PDF) so that book buyers who don't have e-book readers can purchase, download your book to their computer or mobile device and read it off a PDF. Available through Ebookit.com, Love Pour Over Me, can be read in each major electronic format. Keep in mind, that the more formats electronic books are available in, the more book buyers and readers you may gain.

Services Offered
Look for e-book publishers that offer a range of services, including cover design, marketing, copyediting, print on demand and audiobook creation and distribution. Although you may not choose to use all of these services as soon as you publish your e-book, you may want to use more of the services after your book has been on the market for a few weeks. In addition, you can save yourself money by finding out how much it costs to format your e-book before you sign a contract with an e-book publishing company. Compare prices and services.

Royalties
Learn the percentage of royalties that you will be paid on each book sold. For example, some e-book publishers may only deduct 15 percent off the sale of each book it sells direct to consumers, while other companies may deduct a larger percentage. Also, find out if you can sell your e-books on your own website or blog to increase sales.

Considerations

Traditional print book publishers also publish e-books. You may be able to sign a book deal with an established book publisher and get your book published in print, audio and digital format. Also, remember to market and promote your book after it's published by taking steps like writing and sending press releases about your e-book, scheduling radio and television interviews, creating accounts at social media networks and telling your social media account followers about your book and participating in book blog tours.

"Marketing is what you do, not what you say."
-- Andy Sernovitz

Chapter 14 - Getting Books Into Bookstores

The global book publishing industry exceeded $110 billion in 2019. Even with COVID19's impact, the book industry was expected to generate $110.1 billion in revenues in 2020.[16]

If you're a nonfiction book author, particularly an author who writes trade, education or academic textbooks, you might appreciate that these books are major sellers. In fact, Pearson Education, Wolters Kluwer, Bertelsmann SE & Co., Thompson Reuters and RELX Group are major players in the book industry.

Also, when you think about getting your books into bookstores, consider that each of these segments is part of the book publishing industry:

- Trade Books and Other Publications
- Educational Publications
- Academic Books
- Professional Publications
- Consumer Fiction
- Children's Books

More specifically, you could write, publish and sell these types of materials to bookstores:

- Maps
- Dictionaries
- Pamphlets
- Travel Guides
- Novels
- Picture Books
- Technical Manuals
- Encyclopedia
- Academic Textbooks
- Scientific Texts

But you need interest in your book. Librarians, individual book buyers, colleges, universities, military stores and trade groups need to know about your books. They also need to find your books interesting or of enough value to pay for them. And they need to know *where* to get your books.

Each step in <u>Book Marketing That Drives Up Book Sales</u> can help you to generate sufficient interest in your books to arouse the interest of school, trade and bookstore buyers. To get your books in bookstores:

- Study the market (e.g. academic, fiction, children's books) that your book fits
- Familiarize yourself with how the bookstores that you want to sell your books in operate. For instance, do the bookstores buy from Ingram or another distributor? Also, find out the store's return policy.
- Start with local bookstores. This gives you the chance to build your confidence and learn how to communicate with book buyers. Ask to speak with the person who selects books to buy for the store. At a small bookstore, this may be the bookstore owner.
- Ask where you can send an ARC or a copy of the finished book. Visit with the buyer in person, if possible.
- Should the store not green light selling your books on the first pitch, ask if you can conduct a book signing at the store.
- If the store agrees, market the book signing to the hilt. Ask family, friends, colleagues, everyone you know to come to the book signing and to buy one to two copies of your book. This attention might help to get your book on that bookstore's shelves.
- As previously discussed, also get your books in wholesaler and distributor (e.g. Ingram, Baker & Taylor) systems.

- Develop a written marketing plan for your book. This should be a detailed marketing plan. Bookstore buyers might ask to review the plan. As a tip, include current and past sales that you've already generated, the more sales, the better.

Generate a detailed marketing plan that covers social media marketing, book signings, book tours, radio, podcasts, television, blogging and video marketing (to be covered later in <u>Book Marketing That Drives Up Book Sales</u>) and you could sell more books in bookstores, online and elsewhere.

"Marketing isn't magic. There is a science to it."
-- Dan Zarrella

Chapter 15 - Do Press Releases Still Work?

Twenty years ago, press releases got the attention of media pros and consumers. Their stickiness may not be what it was. But press releases are still a way to introduce your book to newspapers, magazines, radio and television stations and book related websites.

You may love that press releases are fairly simple and easy to write. A good way to learn how to write press releases is to read a dozen good press releases. After awhile, writing a book press release may feel like second nature.

Awesome Press Releases Pack Sales Punch

Awesome press releases don't just inform readers. Great press releases pack a recognizable sales punch.
I've seen the numbers of listeners at radio shows like Off The Shelf skyrocket after the radio show ran a press announcement for only two to three shows in a row.

Features in Effective Press Releases

Read these following important elements that are not only a part of awesome press releases but that can give your next releases a rock solid sales punch.

- **Must read headline**. Add words that trigger emotion to your press release headlines. Buffer shares headline formulas. Smart Blogger, Freelance Writing Gigs and My Quick Idea are spots where you can get great words to use in headlines.
- **Focus on the advantages**. Introduce readers to your book's advantages right away. Share the name of your new books from the beginning. If you're sending a press release to announce an event (e.g. book signing, university speaking event), give the name of the event, location and date and time immediately. Then, go right into the benefits that people will gain from attending your event.
- **Expert backup**. Awesome press releases include snippets of a testimonial or feature interviews from one to three industry experts. Thanks to social media, you can reach out to experts for testimonials and short, concise interviews directly from your computer. Don't force people to rely on your word

alone. Give them more proof that what you're saying is accurate.

- **Inform and educate**. List three to five benefits about your book or event (e.g. television appearance, radio interview). Keep each item to five to six words, to force yourself to be as clear as possible. Use a paragraph of to present this information. Write for industry insiders, novices and book buyers.
- **Be honest**. Be honest about your book's features, pricing, product guarantees and return policies. Set high goals that you and your publishing or marketing team can *consistently produce*.
- **Be prepared**. Prepare for consumer response. Staff up to handle customer orders. The last thing that you want is to send a press release that gets national exposure only to discover that you don't have enough books on hand to meet customer demands.

Enhance Press Releases with These Elements

- **Add amazing visuals**. Forget stock images. Take pictures of your books yourself. Shoot for originality. Because they are your pictures, make the images work for you. Use the original pictures in videos, blogs, articles and on your website and social media pages. Definitely add the original pictures that you took yourself to your press releases. Top press release distribution services let you upload pictures when you're submitting media announcements.

- **Keywords**. The right keywords are a must. Press releases need to be found. Professional marketing writers can help you to write press announcements using targeted keywords. Consider using tools like Google Keyword Planner if you're writing your own press releases.
- **Videos**. Create a video so that readers can see your book characters in action. Add a link to your video in your news announcement.
- **Contact information**. Absolutely do not skip this step. You'd be surprised how many people do. Include your contact information at the bottom of your press releases. Details to include with your contact information are: the name of your publishing company, mailing address, website URL, phone number and email address. If your press releases generates the right interest, it could lead to feature interviews and television and radio appearances.

Decide on the right press release distribution service to use. Distribution services that have an international or national reach could yield the best results. Also, keep regional and industry specific press release distribution services in mind. The key is to alert media experts to your latest books and events regularly, at least once a month. Another important key is to choose distribution services that have *real and valuable relationships* with actual magazine and newspaper reporters, media writers, television journalists and digital news professionals.

"Video marketing is another path to your book buyer's door." -- Denise Turney

Chapter 16 - Developing a Video Channel

These simple, easy YouTube tricks can help you to reach more prospects. The tricks can also help you to deepen connections with existing book buyers. Even if you only apply these steps once a week, you can see results. Consistency is key.

Video, Audio and Editing Equipment

There's no promise that you will attract thousands of viewers at your YouTube Channel. But the more work you put into these easy YouTube tricks, the more you could deepen your impact.

If you're new to the world of online videos, to save costs, consider using your laptop or computer camera. If your computer has a good webcam, you should be set.

Ready to upgrade your taping equipment? Think about investing in a quality video and audio recorder. Video editing equipment tends to be pricier. A complete video recording and editing station can run from $1,000 to over $6,000. As an alternative, you could pay for editing software. You can get video editing software for as little as $20. But, again, if you're just starting out and watching expenses, your computer camera can do the job.

Show Viewer's Your Video Channel's Worth
Create a video recording, editing and publishing schedule. Identify and research keywords to use in your video descriptions. This may be one of the most overlooked video marketing tricks.

Search engines love keywords. It's no mystery. People plug in keywords and phrases to find online content. Think of keywords and phrases that your book's audience searches on to find the type of literary content that your video channel provides.

You can get a clue about this by researching top keywords that pull up competitor's videos. Write a three to four paragraph description for each video that you publish. Save yourself time and write enough descriptions to align with several weeks of videos.

If you have keyword SEO tools on your blog, plug keywords into the tool and use relevant results in your video descriptions. Publish videos on different days of the week and at different times of the day. Measure the results to see which publishing schedule works best for you. The more frequently you publish content rich videos, the more traction you may gain from these YouTube video marketing techniques.

Add YouTube Annotations

Enhance YouTube videos with annotations. You'll find annotations under "YouTube Video Manager". Click the "Edit" button for the video that you want to add annotations to. Then, click "Annotations".

Identify where you want to place annotations. For example, you could create "Subscribe to this YouTube Channel" annotations at the start and end of each of your videos. Other annotation examples include the name of the video presenter, your website URL or where viewers can sign up for an upcoming book conference that you're sponsoring.

Market Every Single Video

Market every book video that you make. Post the videos with a teaser message, question or humorous tidbit at your social media channels. Other easy YouTube tricks are to add new videos to your blog, direct emails and literary newsletters.

That means adding your new videos to LinkedIn, Facebook, ScoopIt, Twitter, Mix, Instagram, Tumbler and more. At the beginning and end of your videos, ask viewers to subscribe to your channel. Also, ask viewers to like and share videos that you create.

Comment on popular videos that other people create, especially influencers, book club presidents, publicists, literary agents, etc. who focus on content that is similar to yours. As a note, the more videos that you create, the more of your videos can go into YouTube's rotation. If you've spent an hour watching different YouTube videos, you know that videos will continue to pull up and rotate for you to view until you log out of YouTube. You want as many of your videos to get into rotation as possible.

Get in front of viewers. Take advantage of YouTube and other video platform marketing training sessions. Some of these sessions run for several weeks. Many of the trainings are completely free.

You could partner with companies that provide reasonably priced video marketing services. Make sure that these companies yield "real" results. The Internet is replete with bots and inactive social media followers that marketing companies tap into to make it appear that you're getting more exposure than you actually are.

Another way that you could capitalize on YouTube TV is to study one to three channels that you want to advertise on. Find out which shows your target audience watches. Reach out to peers to share the cost of an ad if you're currently unable to afford the price when you decide to run the ad.

Also, watch the traffic on the free YouTube video network. Be prepared to make content and marketing adjustments should you notice dips in your traffic. For example, you might find that you attract more video viewers when you publish videos on Wednesday mornings at 7am. Or you might find that you gain more video views when you publish new videos on Saturday afternoons between 1pm and 2pm.

"Build relationships where your readers go to know, like and trust you." -- Shelley Hitz

Chapter 17 - Book Marketing During COVID-19

From bookstore closures to postponed writer's conferences, book festivals and live author book signings, COVID-19 is impacting the book industry. Fact is, as solitary as the book industry may seem to be, in order to thrive, bookstore owners, book publishers, literary agents, publicists and authors need to connect with each other as well as with readers.

Book Marketing and COVID-19

The traditional book marketing landscape has definitely changed, thanks to COVID-19. But there are still ways to develop and maintain great connections. This chapter focuses on key ways that you can connect with readers while practicing social distancing.

The point is that book marketing is about more than selling books. In fact, it's while marketing books that you gain the chance to build rewarding face-to-face relationships with book buyers. Especially during book signings, you can ask readers what most appealed to them about your novel, who their favorite fictional characters are and what they'd like to see in upcoming books that you write.

Keep reading to gain 10 tips, real practical actions that you can take, that can help you to win at book marketing, even as we continue to adjust to living with the coronavirus. There's only one tip that you might have to leave your home to finish.

10 Book Marketing Tips Support Social Distancing
The first tip is important for nearly any book marketing situation. In fact, you may want to keep using these tips after the COVID-19 disruption is over:

1. **Create your own book giveaway mailing list.** Looking for ways to do this? Add a "Subscribe Here" button to your website. To receive free books during giveaways, ask website visitors to fill out a form that requires them to provide their email address. Include a box for readers to check, confirming that they agree to receive discount, free and informational content from you.

2. **Host a Facebook Live book reading**. In fact, this is great way to stir up interest in older titles. And it's a

great way to generate interest in your soon-to-be-released novel.

3. **Conduct digital television interviews**. Technology has made it possible to do book interviews on live TV and television streaming channels from your home.

4. **Schedule online radio interviews**. Podcasts like Off The Shelf Books Talk Radio conduct one-hour author feature interviews.

5. **Send electronic holiday greetings**. But don't just send out holiday greetings. Send electronic greetings to targeted recipients (e.g. readers who've purchased one or more books from you, book club presidents, leaders of organizations that work in the field your book is focused in).

6. **Design social media headers**. These are professional headers that attract immediate attention. However, if you don't have solid design skills, consider working with a talented graphics or website designer. But tools like Canva, BookBrush, VistaPrint, etc. can make designing a social media heater a snap.

7. **Order a book marketing magnet for your car**. Place the magnet on your car's bumper or the front or back doors.

8. **Join a cross-author book promotion group**. And, be prepared to share other writers' books with your

contacts. Writers in the group will do the same for your titles.

9. **Introduce your books to private social media groups**. But don't just market your books. Post questions, answer questions and offer tips.

10. **Develop cool book marketing postcards to mail to your contacts**. This is where you may have to leave home and go to the post office. Why? These are print (hold-in-your-hand) postcards. When COVID-19 passes, your post card could stand out when people return to work.

Growing Book Marketing Strategies

Social distancing or not, marketing books is not easy. To be successful, as an author, you have to be committed. This means, that you market your books even if you go days without a book sale. You market books when it's storming outside, you feel like you're wasting time and your outreach yields numerous "no's".

Also, to know which book marketing actions best fit your book, your schedule, travel and financial situation, track your efforts. You'll love that this is as simple as tracking contacts like book clubs, radio stations, newspaper editors, librarians and social media groups on a spreadsheet. Update the spreadsheet with outreach results. For example, did your email to a local radio DJ yield you an interview? If so, log that on the spreadsheet with the date of the interview.

It can be so beneficial. In fact, when a cure for COVID-19 is developed or vaccines reduce the virus' disruption, consider incorporating the above tips into your standard book marketing efforts. Also, stay creative. In other words, keep looking for and developing new, effective ways to find and connect with readers.

"There are those who dream and wish and there are those who dream and work." -- June E. McIntyre

Chapter 18 - Why Use Book Marketing Analytics

Book marketing can be a challenge for authors. This is due, in part, to the fact that authors, particularly novelists, rely on imagination and creativity to develop their works. While writing, creativity, imagination and relying on the muse are blessings, they aren't always blessings during the book marketing process.

Book Marketing Options

In fact, novelists can sink into *magical thinking* after their books are published. Fortunately, there are doors leading from fiction writing to book marketing and book sales. The first door sees fiction writers handing the job of marketing books to publicists, marketing specialists and content marketing writers. But those options cost money.

As a fiction writer, you could go through the second door and use marketing analytics to steer your book marketing efforts. Time may be your greatest investment. It takes time, consistent time, to market books. For example, if you use Amazon Advantage sponsored ads to market your books, download marketing analytics twice a month. But don't just download the reports.

Review the reports. Pay attention to which keywords are getting clicks that turn into book sales. Lower bids on keywords that receive clicks but, no sales. Also, attend free Amazon Advantage sponsored ad webinars. Keep learning. Book marketing tools and platforms change. Attending webinars can keep you abreast of these changes.

Content Marketing Analytics

If you use ebook marketing tools like social media automated marketing platforms (e.g. HootSuite, Buffer, Marketo, InfusionSoft), review marketing analytics associated with those platforms. And make changes based on what the analytics show. Do the same with website content marketing analytics.

In fact, you may want to work with content management systems (CMS) that have robust content marketing analytics. Also, SEO keyword analytics, meta tag description analytics, paragraph length, image alt text, excerpt features and keyword headings are a few features to look for in content marketing analytics.

Another thing, when doing content marketing, perform keyword planning before you start writing landing pages and blog articles. Just make sure that your writing flows, is conversational and reads naturally. Also, focus on providing tips, insight, guidance and entertainment more than focusing on adding SEO keywords to blog articles.

About Digital Marketing Analytics
Digital marketing analytics can keep you from slipping into magical thinking as a novelist. This is an advantage. Why? Magical thinking could find you believing that your novels are going to sell loads of copies *simply* because you wrote the books.

If you don't think that you're doing this, ask yourself why you're not marketing books that you write. And, if you are marketing your books but not receiving lots of book sales, ask yourself why you aren't doing what it takes to increase your book sales -- even while you keep expecting your book sales to suddenly (somehow) pick up.

Marketing analytics can help you to steer clear of magical thinking. The length and depth of this advantage may be unknown. In fact, this advantage, can save you thousands of dollars. Also, it can save you countless hours, frustration and heartache. Really. It can.

But you can't just have digital marketing analytics. You have to review the analytics. See what you need to change and make adjustments. This is an ongoing process. As you start to understand what works for you and take the right book marketing actions, you should see your book sales increase.

Measuring Book Marketing ROI
Staff at book marketing companies aren't shy about telling self-published authors that they have the skills and experience to help increase, perhaps significantly, a book's sales. In fact, if you're a self-published author who has been publishing your own books for five years or more, you've probably crossed paths with book marketing staff members who tried to sell you on the idea that, by working with them, you could sell enough books to afford to write full-time.

Measuring Book Marketing Companies Work

If you believe the hype, you could end up plunking down several hundred or several thousand dollars for press releases, newsletters, brochures, websites and social media book marketing campaigns that don't yield good results. This is just one of the reasons why it's good to do your homework (*before you contract with book marketing companies*) as a self-published author, to get references and check page rankings for websites and press releases that book marketing companies have worked on.

To avoid throwing money away on book marketing campaigns, you can also start measuring book marketing return on investment (ROI). In fact, it's a good practice to measure ROI on all marketing steps that you take. Some tools that you can use to measure book marketing ROI include:

- Customer Surveys (be willing to accept feedback you receive from customers)
- Statistics (i.e. website stats, email marketing stats)
- Google Analytics (track where visitors are coming into your website from, how long they are staying

at your website, website pages that your visitors click to most, etc.)

- Number of interviews you land following the publication of press releases, etc.
- Google Feed Burner (use to monitor the impact of your blog and website feeds)

Tools to Measure Book Marketing Efforts With
Perhaps most importantly, you can measure changes in your book sales. For example, you could check your BarnesandNoble.com and Amazon.com book sales rankings.

In addition, if staff at book marketing companies run social media marketing campaigns for you, consider checking the increases in followers and social media comments and questions that you receive.

Not only could measuring book marketing ROI save you money, it could also help you to spot opportunities for improvement and growth. It could alert you to areas of your book marketing campaigns that you should tweak, stop or focus on more. Measuring book marketing ROI could also keep you from deceiving yourself into believing that, just because you are working hard, you're yielding good results.

Every Book Author Has an Audience

As a piggyback on the importance of using and reviewing book marketing analytics, it's important to remember that there is an audience for your book. In fact, Emily Dickinson may not have gone out of her way to publish and market her written works while she walked the earth, yet, after her sister discovered and started marketing her poems, *her work found its audience.*

People began buying her poetry, even discussing it at schools and in writer's groups. This happening may point to the fact that every author, be they aware of it or not, has an audience, a group of readers who are eager to explore, examine and enjoy the books, stories or poems that they write.

When to Start Finding Your Reading Audience

However, if you're an author, the time to ponder or try to figure out who you're writing for might not be during the creative process. I say this because my experience has been that great art comes from within the artist, not from a strategy to sell lots of books. The success of Emily

Dickinson's poetry and Vincent Van Gogh's paintings may prove this.

If you create with sincerity, after you publish and market your works, you may discover that people from certain backgrounds, age groups, etc. buy and appreciate your books most. You can discover this whether you sell 100 books or 25 million books. As you develop conversations with these people, responding to their inquiries and comments, don't be surprised if these members of your reading audience start asking when your next book is scheduled to be published or if you plan on writing a sequel to your recent novel.

Of course, you can also take the traditional marketing approach and research a segment of the general population, learn what their passions and interests are and write stories that meet their interests. However, if your work feels forced (as if you are merely writing to get book sales from a certain demographic) readers may catch on. Your stories also might lack sincerity.

You also might not appreciate the creative process. Because it is during the creative process that authors often reap their greatest rewards as they tap into hidden truths, emotions, perceptions and beliefs about themselves.

Finding Your Reading Audience
After you finish creating a story, to find your reading audience you may want to follow the route Emily Dickinson took and let someone else spread the word about your books. You can do this by hiring a marketing firm or publicists to tell the media and reading public about your books.

Should you decide to market and promote your books yourself, you can connect with readers on social media. You can also blog and write columns for periodicals that reach the types of people you think would love to hang out with your book characters were they real people. When using the column writing approach, always be sure to include your name, book title and website URL in your byline.

If you plan on writing several books, consider building a database that includes the names and contact information of readers who purchase your books directly from you or email you, requesting that you keep them updated on your writings.

"Not everything that counts can be counted. You can count sales. You can count fans and followers. You can count pins and tweets. But you can't count passion. You can't count commitment. You can't count engagement. You can't count relationships." -- John Kremer

Chapter 19 - Non-Bookstore Marketing

Bookstores and the Internet aren't the only places where you can sell books. In fact, you can sell books right outside the trunk of your car. You can also sell books at a mall pop-up store.

Land speaking engagements at colleges and universities and you can set up a table and sell books right after the speaking event. Speaking events was one of my big ways to sell books when I was starting out.

During those early days, I'd register to appear at city, and regional events as a keynote speaker, panelist or guests. Was I ever nervous during those initial speaking events.

Rather than to talk myself out of taking the stage, I focused on the rewards of connecting with people in the audience. I focused on building relationships.

After speaking at half a dozen events, I came to love public speaking. It's a good way to know organizers of book conferences, book festivals and trade shows. Public speaking is also a good way to become known as an "expert" or a "professional" in the eyes of event attendees.

Another advantage of using public speaking to market books has to do with sheer numbers. Each person who signs up for the public speaking event (e.g. lecture, seminar, motivational speech) is a present and potential book buyer. In fact, after you take the stage and just before you walk off stage, let attendees know that they can get a copy of the book that you're referencing during your speech if they come to the back of the stage (or wherever the signing is) right after the event.

Also, ask these attendees to sign up for your literary newsletter. Make it easy for them to do this by bringing a clipboard and a printed sign-up sheet to the event.

More non-bookstore marketing spots include street festivals and flea markets (some people generate a full-time income selling products at flea markets). Here's a list of even more non-bookstore marketing places:

- Book Festivals (You may have to buy a booth. But you'll have an audience of avid book buyers. Take advantage of these opportunities.)
- Book Conferences (Ask to speak on a panel or as a keynote speaker. You might get your registration fee, hotel or travel paid for if you ask.)
- Cultural Events (Strive for large cultural events, the types of events that attract 5,000 or more attendees. This puts you in front of thousands of potential book buyers.)
- Retail Stores (These are stores that sell products that align with your book's topic. For example, if you wrote a book about fishing, contact sports and outdoors store owners and ask if you can sell your books in their shops.)
- Gift Shops (Hospital gift shops carry a range of books, including fiction and nonfiction. Start with local gift shops and branch out.)
- Secondary Schools (Children's books may perform better with elementary schools. Find out who the school's book buyer is. Write this person and send her or him your book ARC.)
- Trade and corporate organizations (Depending on your book's topic, you could sell bulk copies of your

book to professional associations, trade organizations, etc.)

- Military Exchanges (Large military bases have exchange stores. Similar to department stores, you can buy books, groceries, clothes, toys and other goods at exchanges. According to The Exchange, "The majority of books and publications are supplied to exchanges by local distributors serving the area in which the exchange is located." Furthermore, "For selling books and publications within the Exchange, contact the specific distributor with questions regarding item selection and purchasing procedures."[17]

Taking Books on Successful Road Trips

Hitting the road and going on book tours is an effective way to connect with readers in person, answering their questions about your writing process, characters in your books and what inspired or motivated you to create the stories you've penned. By taking your books on the road you can also increase your book sales in the short and long term.

Map out road trips. These are different than a book tour. For example, you might budget to attend four large book festivals and two large cultural festivals that are spread across 12-months. Also, create a budget for these road trips and stick to that budget.

Get the Most Out of Book Road Trips

Readers appreciate meeting the authors who write their favorite books. In this regard, readers are akin to sports and music fans. They want to get close to the people who use their talents to captivate, entertain, inspire, educate and/or motivate them. Truth be told, many of us book authors, who are also avid book readers, get excited when we meet other writers whose works we admire.

Plus, book events are fun. Take events like the Maui Writer's Conference, Jaipur Literary Festival, Shanghai Literary Festival, Sydney Writer's Festival, International Festival of Authors or the Miami International Book Festival and its clear to see why millions of people trek out to book events each year. There are author discussion panels, editor and literary agent meet and greets, keynote speakers and, of course, book signings.

To get the most out of book road trips, consider creating an itinerary so that you remember to visit certain booths, connect with media and engage readers while you're out and about. You can also:

- Introduce yourself to event organizers (it's a great way to learn about upcoming appearance opportunities)
- Schedule interviews with talk radio stations within 15 or fewer miles of the book event you're attending
- Bring enough books to sell at local events that you're scheduled to attend
- Visit other author booths (it's a great way to network and make friends)
- Focus on building relationships with book lovers (keep in mind that if you don't sell lots of books at an event, if you make enough rewarding connections, you may see an increase in book sales days or weeks after you return home)
- Giveaway free bookmarks, brochures, book excerpts, etc. (be sure to include your website URL on all giveaways)
- Volunteer to read from your books at events

At the end of the events be sure to thank the event organizers, supporters and book lovers for coming. In fact, make it a point to thank each person who stops by your booth, even if they don't buy a copy of your book. I made a point to do this while on the road with my books. I plan on taking my newest books, <u>Love Pour Over Me</u> and <u>Rosetta The Talent Show Queen</u>, on the road during 2021 and 2022. Hope to see you while I'm on the road!

While you're on the road with your books, meeting readers, media, booksellers and librarians, remember that life is truly about communicating and relationships. Above all, love what you're doing. Stay in the moment and allow yourself to absolutely love and enjoy attending each book event you travel to!

Funding the Early Stages of a Writing Career
Your dreams of striking it big as a writer might take a few months, or years, to manifest. Before your dreams manifest, sitting in front of a computer screen, creating cliff hanging scenes, may not generate enough income for you to pay all your expenses. To keep moving forward, you're going to have to find a way to fund your writing career.

Ways to Generate Income as a Book Author

Some obvious ways that you can fund the early stages of your writing career include getting a full-time or part-time job or starting an online business and selling digital products or services. If you want to have enough time to continue developing interesting nonfiction books, novel plots, unforgettable characters and engaging dialogue, consider getting a part-time job or a full-time job that doesn't require you to work 10 hours a day or weekends. You could also start freelance writing for business clients, people who are looking for professional writers to help them market and sell their products and services.

Other steps that you could take to fund the early stages of your writing career are:

- Blogging (setting up your own blog using platforms like WordPress, Bravehost, etc. and adding affiliate ads to your blog so that you can start earning money)
- Teaching writing courses (you could teach a writing course at a local community college or you could start your own online writing course, asking attendees to pay a fee to attend webinars, etc. that you lead)

- Advertising business products (if you start your own radio show, you could reach out to businesses and establish marketing arrangements with them where they pay you a certain amount of money a month to advertise their products or services on your radio show)
- Writing non-fiction articles and feature interviews for magazines, newspapers and journals (resources like Media Bistro, Indeed, Freelance Writing Jobs, Journalism Jobs, etc. post writing job openings)
- Edit other novelists' manuscripts (I know of a few people who have earned money doing this; it's another way to stay close to writing while you earn an income)

Each of these steps does more than help you start generating additional income. These steps also allow you to continue to use and sharpen your writing skills. For example, if you worked as a copywriter, you could earn $50 an hour, developing banner ads, print ads, video and radio scripts, brochures and blog posts for clients. As you complete your writing assignments, you could also learn new ways to work with editors and strengthen your time management skills so that you always meet deadlines.

You could also discover new ways to market your books, something that will definitely benefit you as you continue to move your writing career forward.

There are many ways to market your books. In fact, there are so many ways to market and sell books online, offline, in bookstores and at non-bookstore locations that you may want to build a street team to help market your books.

Another option is to work with a book marketing company that could handle your social media book marketing. You could also hire a freelancer to manage scheduling radio, podcasts and television interviews for you.

Start small and build out. Find which book marketing tools and techniques generate the most book sales for you. I'm pulling for you.

"Thinking outside of the box and watching for opportunities that look like a good fit are some avenues that have helped me generate publicity."
-- Barbara Techel

Chapter 20 - Book Marketing Resources

Although I shared online and offline book marketing resources throughout the chapters in <u>Book Marketing That Drives Up Book Sales</u>, here are even more resources that you could use to market and sell books. One thing may be certain. There's always another way to market and sell books.

1. **BookBub.com -** Major, mid-list and new authors advertise on Book Bub. Feature ads can start around $300. But you can also advertise your book for impressions or clicks across a time period that you set for a rate you choose.
2. **Book Circle** - Author interviews and book discussions - http://www.bookcircleonline.com
3. **Book Lover's Haven** - Free literary magazine that you could get featured in founded by yours truly - https://www.chistell.com/newsletter.html
4. **BookTalk.org** - You can advertise your book for a low annual fee. BookTalk.org has been around for 18 years.

In addition to advertising, they have free discussion forums.

5. **Douglas Coleman Show** - Podcast - Entertainment, books, etc. focus - https://www.douglascolemanmusic.com

6. **Electric Literature** - Indie Literary Magazines - https://electricliterature.com/10-indie-literary-magazines-you-should-be-reading/

7. **Help a Reporter Out (HARO)** - Subscribe to stay aware of topics that media personnel want to interview a guest for. If you book, public speaking background, passions align with the HARO request, you could land an interview - https://www.helpareporter.com/

8. **Hubspot.com** - Free marketing guides, etc.

9. **Kikwetu Journal** - Journal of East African Literature - https://www.kikwetujournal.com/

10. **Kindlepreneur** - Places to market and promote free Kindle books - https://kindlepreneur.com/list-sites-promote-free-amazon-books/

11. **Lifestyles with Tia** - Podcast - Focus on inspirational stories, entertainment and relationship topics - anchor.fm/tiaspage

12. **Neon Books** - UK Literary Magazines - https://www.neonbooks.org.uk/big-list-literary-magazines/

13. **Newswire.com** - Press Release Distribution Service

14. **Off The Shelf** - Free author, editor, screenplay writer, publicists, etc. radio interview. Off The Shelf has been around for more than 12 years. Contact me if you'd like to schedule an interview. Reach out early; the show books up fast. - https://www.blogtalkradio.com/denise-turney-
15. **Poets & Writers** - Author interviews, writing contests, book events, grants and awards, writer retreats and more - https://www.pw.org/
16. **PRWeb.com** - Press Release Distribution Service
17. **Publisher's Weekly** - Publishing and Marketing info - https://www.publishersweekly.com/pw/by-topic/industry-news/publishing-and-marketing/index.html
18. **Radio Guest List** - List more than 100 podcast and radio stations that you could interview on - https://www.radioguestlist.com/
19. **Reedsy** - List Book Promotion Sites, Book Editors, Literary Magazines, Writing Contests and more - https://reedsy.com/
20. **Rock Your World Naturally** - Podcast - Health and Wellness focus - https://tinyurl.com/y896zcte
21. **Storiad** - Book Marketing Platform (Do your homework before paying for any marketing service with any vendor.) - https://storiad.com

22. **The Writer** - Literary Journals and Magazines - https://www.writermag.com/market-directory/literary-magazine/

23. **2021 Upcoming Writing / Book Events** - https://www.chistell.com/upcoming-writing-book-events.html

24. **Website Hosting Services** - List website hosting services with prices. Adding so you can get a glimpse of services, prices to compare when searching for a website hosting service - https://www.cnet.com/news/best-web-hosting/

25. **Web Hosting Buddy** - Larger list of website hosting services (prices aren't readily highlighted) - https://webhostingbuddy.com/list-of-web-hosting-companies/

26. **2021 Writer Conferences** - https://thewritelife.com/writers-conferences/

27. **Written Word Media** - https://www.writtenwordmedia.com. They run separate newsletter ads for free books, newly released books, discounted books romance and reading stacks. Generally, you have to wait 30 days to run a new ad on the same book.

References

1. United States Copyright Office. Accessed December 21, 2020.
2. United States Library of Congress. Pre-assigned Control Number Program. Accessed December 21, 2020.
3. The Daily Egg. The 15 Second Rule: 3 Reasons Why Visitors Leave a Website. Accessed December 23, 2020.
4. PodcastInsights. 2020 Podcast Stats & Facts (New Research From Oct2020). Updated October 6, 2020. Accessed December 24, 2020.
5. Statista. Most Popular Social Networking Apps In The United States as of September 2019, By Monthly Users. Accessed December 25, 2020.
6. Facebook Help Center. Can I see who's seen each post in a Facebook group I admin? Accessed December 25, 2020.
7. AdExpresso by Hootsuite. Ana Gotter. The 27 Facebook Statistics That Every Marketer Must Know To Win In 2021. Published December 16, 2020. Accessed December 25, 2020.
8. Brandwatch. Kit Smith. 60 Incredible and Interesting Twitter Stats and Statistics. Published January 2, 2020. Accessed December 25, 2020.
9. Oberlo. Tik Tok Statistics. Accessed December 25, 2020.
10. Buffer. How The Instagram Algorithm Works In 2019: Everything You Need To Know. Accessed December 25, 2020.
11. Hubspot. Emily Coates. 77 Essential Social Media Marketing Statistics for 2020. Accessed December 25, 2020.
12. Blogging Wizard. The Best Social Media Scheduling Tools for 2020. Accessed December 25, 2020.
13. Penguin Random House. The State of the Book Club. Accessed December 25, 2020.

14. AARP. Ken Budd. 9 Online Book Clubs You Can Join Now. Published May 12, 2020. Accessed December 26, 2020.
15. American Booksellers Association. Baker & Taylor to Drop Wholesale Book Distribution to Retailers. Published May 8, 2019. Accessed December 26, 2020.
16. IBIS World. Global Book Publishing Industry. Published August 31, 2020. Accessed December 26, 2020.
17. Exchange. Retail Sales. Accessed December 26, 2020.

Books Written by Denise Turney
Love Pour Over Me
Spiral
Love Has Many Faces
Portia
Long Walk Up
Awaken Blessings of Inner Love
Rosetta The Talent Show Queen
Running Toward Freedom
Book Marketing That Drives Up Book Sales
Heal Gorgeous: Wisdom Within You Knows The Way

www.ingramcontent.com/pod-product-compliance
Lightning Source LLC
Chambersburg PA
CBHW070230180526
45158CB00001BA/335